The Wild Side

TOTAL PANIC

The Wild Side

TOTAL PANIC

Henry Billings

Melissa Billings

JAMESTOWN PUBLISHERS

a division of NTC/CONTEMPORARY PUBLISHING GROUP

Lincolnwood, Illinois USA

ISBN 0–8092-9512-1

Published by Jamestown Publishers,
a division of NTC/Contemporary Publishing Group, Inc.
4255 West Touhy Avenue,
Lincolnwood (Chicago), Illinois 60712-1975, U.S.A.
2 3 4 5 6 7 8 9 10 11 12 113 09 08 07 06 05 04 03 02 01

CONTENTS

UNIT THREE

To the Student

Human beings have a strong instinct for self-preservation. When confronted by a situation that threatens their safety, they naturally plan ways to lessen the danger. When confronted with a situation over which they have no control, their fear escalates into panic. The need to escape the life-threatening danger becomes the only thing on their minds. Unreasoning, senseless, instinctual fear takes over. The articles in this book describe 15 different instances in which everyday people felt panic. Explosions, fires, shark attacks, volcanoes, viruses, and riots are some of the catastrophes that evoke panic in these people, whose lives are suddenly in desperate jeopardy. Perhaps you will agree that the only sensible thing to do in these situations is panic.

As you read and enjoy the 15 articles in this book, you will be developing your reading skills. If you complete all the lessons, you will surely increase your reading speed and improve your reading comprehension and critical thinking skills. Also, because these exercises include items of the types often found on state and national tests, learning how to complete them will prepare you for tests you may have to take in the future.

How to Use This Book

About the Book. *Total Panic* contains three units, each of which includes five lessons. Each lesson begins with an article about an unusual subject or event. The article is followed by a group of four reading comprehension exercises and three critical thinking exercises. The reading comprehension exercises will help you understand the article. The critical thinking exercises will help you think about what you have read and how it relates to your own experience.

At the end of each lesson, you will also have the opportunity to give your personal response to some aspect of the article and then to assess how well you understood what you read.

The Sample Lesson. Working through the sample lesson, the first lesson in the book, with your class or group will demonstrate how a lesson is organized. The sample lesson explains how to complete the exercises and score your answers. The correct answers for the sample exercises and sample scores are printed in lighter type. In some cases, explanations of the correct answers are given. The explanations will help you understand how to think through these question types.

If you have any questions about how to complete the exercises or score them, this is the time to get the answers.

Working Through Each Lesson. Begin each lesson by looking at the photograph and reading the caption. Before you read, predict what you think the article will be about. Then read the article.

Sometimes your teacher may decide to time your reading. Timing helps you keep track of and increase your reading speed. If you have been timed, enter your reading time in the box at the end of the lesson. Then use the Words-per-Minute Table to find your reading speed, and record your speed on the Reading Speed Graph at the end of the unit.

Next complete the Reading Comprehension and Critical Thinking exercises. The directions for each exercise will tell you how to mark your answers. When you have finished all four Reading Comprehension exercises, use the answer key provided by your teacher to check your work. Follow the directions after each exercise to find your score. Record your Reading Comprehension scores on the graph at the end of each unit. Then check your answers to the Author's Approach, Summarizing and Paraphrasing, and Critical Thinking exercises. Fill in the Critical Thinking Chart at the end of each unit with your evaluation of your work and comments about your progress.

At the end of each unit you will also complete a Compare and Contrast Chart. The completed chart will help you see what the articles have in common, and it will give you an opportunity to explore your own ideas about the events in the articles.

SAMPLE
LESSON

Smoke, Fire, and Death

"Fire! Fire!"

2   The cries echoed through the hallways of the 26-story hotel in Las Vegas, Nevada. On the 24th floor, Donald and Janet Tebbutt leaped out of bed. Donald pulled back the drapes and looked out the hotel window. All he could see was thick smoke billowing up from below. Frightened, he and his wife ran out into the hallway. There, they met swarms of other guests. All were looking for the best way out. No one knew whether to go down the stairs or up to the roof. It was a scene of utter chaos.

3   The Tebbutts tried to make their way down the stairs. But the smoke in the stairway was simply too heavy. Turning around, they headed up toward the roof. But the stairway was becoming jammed with people. And the fumes and smoke were making it harder and harder to breathe.

4   As it turned out, the door to the roof was locked. There were windows, but they were lined with steel mesh and unbreakable. For a minute, it looked as though everyone in the stairwell was trapped. Then a man threw himself at the door. It popped open. People poured out onto the roof, gulping in fresh air.

5   All this happened on November 21, 1980. About 7:00 A.M. a kitchen fire broke out in the MGM Grand Hotel in Las Vegas. The flames melted the alarm control box. Because of that, no alarm ever rang. The fire caught all 4,500 guests by surprise. There were other problems as well. None of the guest rooms had smoke detectors. And only the basement, first floor, and top floor had water sprinklers. "More sprinklers would have made all the difference in the world," a firefighter later said.

6   Police and fire trucks rushed to the scene. But the tallest rescue ladder reached only to the ninth floor. Everyone higher up was stranded. Many people climbed out onto their balconies. The police urged them to stay calm. Using bullhorns, police shouted, "Don't jump! Don't jump! The fire is under control!"

7   But one woman couldn't wait. She tied bedsheets together to make a rope. Then she crawled out her 19th floor window and headed down on the makeshift rope. She made it to the 17th floor. Then she lost her grip and fell to her death.

8   Meanwhile, some guests were trapped in the halls. Many were overcome by the smoke. They slumped against walls, gasping for breath. Some people stayed in their rooms. A few wisely soaked towels and used them to block the smoke from seeping under the doors. "If they had stayed in their rooms until we got them," said Fire Chief Ralph Dinsman, "a lot of the dead would have survived."

A kitchen fire at Las Vegas's MGM Grand Hotel went out of control on the morning of November 21, 1980, causing fear and panic among the hotel's 4,500 guests.

9   About 200 people made it to the roof. Rescue helicopters swooped down to get them. But the helicopters could take only a few people at a time. Everyone wanted to be the first to leave. People started pushing and shoving. Luckily, someone in the crowd was a police officer. He pulled out his gun and yelled, "Stand back and keep cool or I will shoot." It worked. Everyone stepped back to wait his or her turn. Before long, all the people on the roof were rescued.

10   Others were not so lucky. When the fire broke out, some gamblers didn't want to leave the first floor casino. They wanted to roll the dice or deal the cards one more time. The employees insisted on leaving. But 10 people stayed behind to scoop up their money and chips. All 10 died in the flames.

11   It wasn't the fire, however, that killed the most people. It was the smoke. The flames never got beyond the second floor. But black smoke funneled up the stairways to all 26 floors. Some people died in bed. One couple was found lying arm in arm. A waiter who had come to serve them breakfast lay dead on the floor beside them. In all, more than 700 people were injured and 84 people died. Kevin Beverton was one who made it out alive. When asked about the fire, he described it this way: "It was death, absolute death there."

If you have been timed while reading this article, enter your reading time below. Then turn to the Words-per-Minute Table on page 55 and look up your reading speed (words per minute). Enter your reading speed on the graph on page 56.

Reading Time: Sample Lesson

———— : ————

Minutes   *Seconds*

A Finding the Main Idea

One statement below expresses the main idea of the article. One statement is too general, or too broad. The other statement explains only part of the article; it is too narrow. Label the statements using the following key:

M—Main Idea   **B—Too Broad**   **N—Too Narrow**

<u> B </u>   1. Skyscrapers should always be equipped with smoke detectors and sprinker systems in case of fire. [This statement is too broad. It doesn't mention where or when this fire took place. It doesn't describe the fire.]

<u> N </u>   2. Helicopters rescued about 200 people who made it to the roof of the hotel. [This statement is true, but it is too narrow. It gives only one piece, or detail, from the article.]

<u> M </u>   3. All 4,500 guests were affected by a terrible fire that roared through the MGM Grand Hotel in Las Vegas in 1980. [This statement is the main idea. It tells when and where the fire took place and how many people were affected by it.]

<u> 15 </u>   Score 15 points for a correct M answer.

<u> 10 </u>   Score 5 points for each correct B or N answer.

<u> 25 </u>   **Total Score:** Finding the Main Idea

B Recalling Facts

How well do you remember the facts in the article? Put an X in the box next to the answer that correctly completes each statement about the article.

1. The MGM Grand Hotel in Las Vegas had
   - ☐ a. five stories.
   - ☒ b. 26 stories.
   - ☐ c. 98 stories.

2. The fire broke out first in the hotel's
   - ☒ a. kitchen.
   - ☐ b. lobby.
   - ☐ c. elevator.

3. The hotel's alarm never rang because
   - ☐ a. its battery was dead.
   - ☐ b. the room it was in was not affected.
   - ☒ c. the alarm control box had melted.

4. Some guests survived by soaking towels and putting them
   - ☒ a. under their doors to keep smoke out.
   - ☐ b. around their heads.
   - ☐ c. over their clothing before they went into the hall.

5. Most of those who died
   - ☐ a. were burned by the flames.
   - ☐ b. were frightened to death.
   - ☒ c. inhaled too much smoke.

Score 5 points for each correct answer.

<u> 25 </u>   **Total Score:** Recalling Facts

C | Making Inferences

When you combine your own experience with information from a text to draw a conclusion that is not directly stated in that text, you are making an inference. Below are five statements that may or may not be inferences based on information in the article. Label the statements using the following key:

C—Correct Inference   **F—Faulty Inference**

_F_ 1. You can be sure that any hotel you visit today will have a working sprinkler system. [This is a *faulty* inference. You can't be sure of this unless you ask.]

_C_ 2. Police officers are trained to be calm and organized in any crisis. [This is a *correct* inference. Part of a police officer's job is maintaining order in crisis.]

_F_ 3. You are more likely to survive a crisis if you adopt a selfish attitude. [This is a *faulty* inference. It was only after guests on the roof began to cooperate that they were rescued.]

_C_ 4. Greed can harm a person's good judgment. [This is a *correct* inference. Ten gamblers stayed behind and died because of their greed.]

_F_ 5. If people had all cooperated in escaping the hotel, no one would have died. [This is a *faulty* inference. Some people died in bed without a chance to cooperate in their rescue.]

Score 5 points for each correct answer.

_25_ **Total Score:** Making Inferences

D | Using Words Precisely

Each numbered sentence below contains an underlined word or phrase from the article. Following the sentence are three definitions. One definition is closest to the meaning of the underlined word. One definition is opposite or nearly opposite. Label those two definitions using the following key; do not label the remaining definition.

C—Closest   **O—Opposite or Nearly Opposite**

1. All he could see was thick smoke <u>billowing up</u> from below.
____ a. playing
_C_ b. rising in wavelike puffs
_O_ c. shooting up rapidly with great force

2. It was a scene of <u>utter</u> chaos.
_O_ a. partial
____ b. sorrowful
_C_ c. complete; total

3. Then she crawled out her 19th floor window and headed down on the <u>makeshift</u> rope.
_C_ a. temporary; substitute
_O_ b. permanent
____ c. heavy

4. But black smoke <u>funneled</u> up the stairways to all 26 floors.
____ a. dried
_O_ b. spread out
_C_ c. moved as through a pipe or channel

5. When asked about the fire, he described it this way: "It was death, <u>absolute</u> death there."

_____C_____ a. unquestionable

_____ b. private

_____O_____ c. possible

__15__	Score 3 points for each correct C answer.
__10__	Score 2 points for each correct O answer.
__25__	**Total Score:** Using Words Precisely

Enter the four total scores in the spaces below, and add them together to find your Reading Comprehension Score. Then record your score on the graph on page 57.

Score	Question Type	Sample Lesson
__25__	Finding the Main Idea	
__25__	Recalling Facts	
__25__	Making Inferences	
__25__	Using Words Precisely	
__100__	**Reading Comprehension Score**	

Author's Approach

Put an X in the box next to the correct answer.

1. What do the authors mean by the statement "It was a scene of utter chaos"?

☐ a. The situation was frightening.

☒ b. The hotel guests did not know where to go or what to do next.

☐ c. The hotel guests were angry.

2. Judging by statements from the article "Smoke, Fire, and Death," you can conclude that the authors want the reader to think that

☐ a. the gamblers who refused to leave had made a wise decision.

☒ b. smoke detectors and more sprinklers probably would have saved lives.

☐ c. the MGM Grand Hotel was well prepared for a fire.

3. What do the authors imply by saying "[The gamblers] wanted to roll the dice or deal the cards one more time"?

☒ a. The gamblers didn't believe they were in serious danger.

☐ b. The gamblers didn't know there was a fire.

☐ c. The gamblers were braver than most other guests.

4. The authors probably wrote this article to

☐ a. discourage people from staying in hotels with more than nine floors.

☒ b. tell about an event that caused fear and panic.

☐ c. show how destructive a fire can be.

__4__	Number of correct answers

Record your personal assessment of your work on the Critical Thinking Chart on page 58.

Summarizing and Paraphrasing

Follow the directions provided for question 1. Put an X in the box next to the correct answer for question 2.

1. Complete the following one-sentence summary of the article using the lettered phrases from the phrase bank below. Write the letters on the lines.

> ### Phrase Bank
> a. how the fire started, how guests reacted to the emergency, and how firefighters rescued victims
> b. a summary of the death and destruction the fire caused
> c. how Donald and Janet Tebbutt tried to escape the fire

The article "Smoke, Fire, and Death" begins with _____c_____, goes on to explain _____a_____, and ends with _____b_____.

2. Read the statement from the article below. Then read the paraphrase of that statement. Choose the reason that best tells why the paraphrase does not say the same thing as the statement.

Statement: The fire chief said that if guests had simply stayed in their rooms and waited to be rescued, more people would have survived the fire.

Paraphrase: According to the fire chief, all the guests would have survived if they had just waited in their rooms.

☐ a. Paraphrase says too much.

☐ b. Paraphrase doesn't say enough.

☒ c. Paraphrase doesn't agree with the statement. [The fire chief didn't say that everyone would have lived, only that more would have survived.]

> ____2____ Number of correct answers
>
> Record your personal assessment of your work on the Critical Thinking Chart on page 58.

Critical Thinking

Follow the directions provided for questions 1, 2, and 3. Put an X in the box next to the correct answer for the other questions.

1. For each statement below, write O if it expresses an opinion or write F if it expresses a fact.

   __F__ a. None of the guest rooms at the MGM Grand Hotel had smoke detectors.

   __O__ b. No one would have been hurt in the MGM Grand fire if there had been smoke detectors in every room.

   __F__ c. One woman died after losing her grip on a rope made of bedsheets tied together.

2. Choose from the letters below to correctly complete the following statement. Write the letters on the lines.

   On the positive side, __b__, but on the negative side, __a__.

   a. 84 people died in the fire

   b. helicopters were able to rescue about 200 people from the hotel roof

   c. there were 4,500 guests at the MGM Grand Hotel on November 21, 1980

3. Choose from the letters below to correctly complete the following statement. Write the letters on the lines.

   According to the article, ___b___ caused the alarm box to

   ___a___, and the effect was ___c___.

   a. melt

   b. a kitchen fire

   c. no alarm ever rang to warn guests about the fire

4. How is "Smoke, Fire, and Death" related to the theme of *Total Panic*?

   ☒ a. Guests at the MGM Grand Hotel panicked while trying to escape a fire at the hotel.

   ☐ b. More than 700 people were injured and 84 were killed in the fire at the MGM Grand Hotel.

   ☐ c. Most floors in the MGM Grand Hotel had no sprinklers to put out the fire.

5. What did you have to do to answer question 3?

   ☒ a. find an effect (something that happened)

   ☐ b. find an opinion (what someone thinks about something)

   ☐ c. find a comparison (how things are the same)

   ___5___ Number of correct answers

   Record your personal assessment of your work on the Critical Thinking Chart on page 58.

Personal Response

I wonder why _____

___[On the lines, complete the sentence with a thought or question that___

___occurred to you while you read the article or after you finished reading it.___

___You may wonder, for example, why there were no smoke detectors or___

___sprinklers in the rooms or why one woman decided to climb down on her___

___bedsheet rope.]___

Self-Assessment

From reading this article, I have learned _____

___[Choose one fact or idea that you learned from this article and___

___write it on the lines.]___

_____

_____

Self-Assessment

To get the most out of the *Wild Side* series, you need to take charge of your own progress in improving your reading comprehension and critical thinking skills. Here are some of the features that help you work on those essential skills.

Reading Comprehension Exercises. Complete these exercises immediately after reading the article. They help you recall what you have read, understand the stated and implied main ideas, and add words to your working vocabulary.

Critical Thinking Skills Exercises. These exercises help you focus on the authors' approach and purpose, recognize and generate summaries and paraphrases, and identify relationships between ideas.

Personal Response and Self-Assessment. Questions in this category help you relate the articles to your personal experience and give you the opportunity to evaluate your understanding of the information in that lesson.

Compare and Contrast Charts. At the end of each unit you will complete a Compare and Contrast Chart. The completed chart helps you see what the articles have in common and gives you an opportunity to explore your own ideas about the topics discussed in the articles.

The Graphs. The graphs and charts at the end of each unit enable you to keep track of your progress. Check your graphs regularly with your teacher. Decide whether your progress is satisfactory or whether you need additional work on some skills. What types of exercises are you having difficulty with? Talk with your teacher about ways to work on the skills in which you need the most practice.

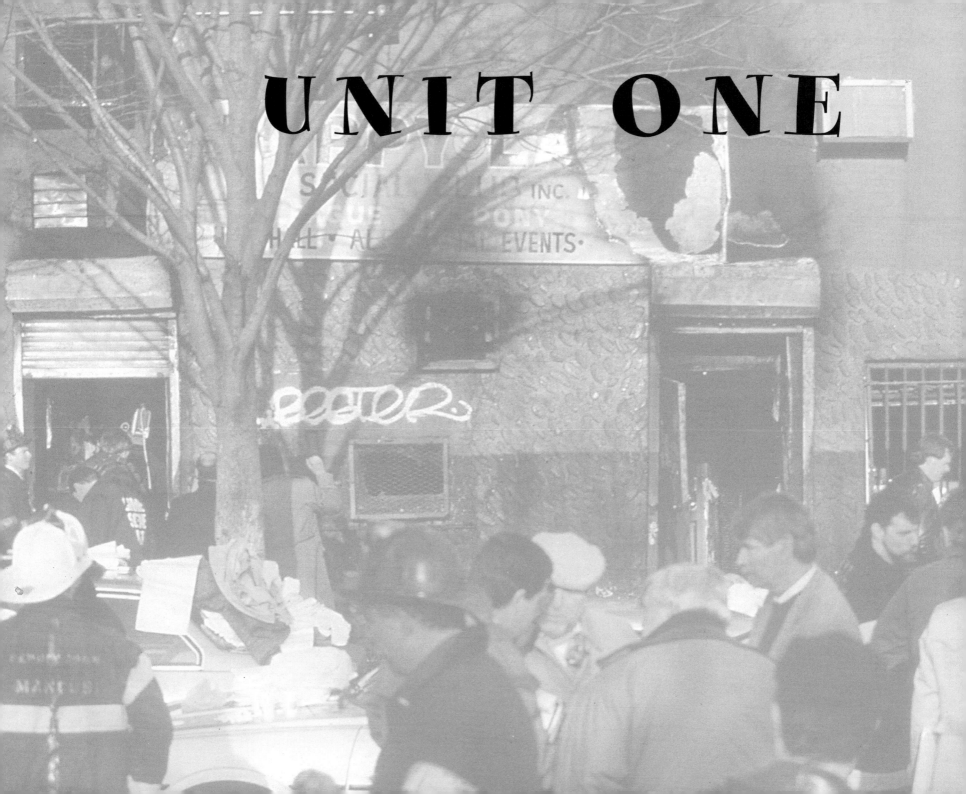

UNIT ONE

An Unexpected Explosion

Most people in Edison, New Jersey, did not even know it was there. And why should they? The natural gas pipeline made no noise. It couldn't be seen. It was buried seven feet underground. For 33 years, this pipeline had done its job silently and without incident. It carried gas from Texas to the Northeast. Ten million homes got fuel from it. It was like a good neighbor—quiet and helpful.

2   But on March 23, 1994, the pipeline made its presence known in an awful way. At 11:58 P.M., it blew up. The

These ruins are all that remained of the Durham Woods Apartments in Edison, New Jersey, after a nearby pipeline exploded. The terrific blast woke residents and sent them running for their lives. The intense heat even melted parked cars.

blast occurred near the Durham Woods Apartments. More than 1,500 people lived there. The explosion was deafening. It blew a hole in the ground 120 feet wide and 60 feet deep. A huge tower of flames shot 400 feet into the air. It turned the sky a bright orange. The flames could be seen 30 miles away in New York City.

3   The people of Edison had no idea what had hit them. Was it a thunderstorm? A tornado? A rocket attack? "I thought it was the end of the world," said Barbara Barone.

4   She wasn't alone. Many other people thought the same thing. Said Kim Krajniak, "My first thought was 'It's a nuclear bomb. We're dead.'" Terrence Reed called his father in nearby Piscataway to tell him that a nuclear bomb had been dropped.

5   The blast awakened everyone in the area. People jumped out of bed and ran for their lives. Many carried pets or babies under their arms. Some were so frightened that they didn't stop to put on clothes. Others grabbed coats or sweaters against the evening chill. As it turned out, they didn't need them. The heat from the blaze was a searing

1000° F. A few people took flashlights. But they didn't need those, either. The orange light was brighter than the noonday sun.

6   The residents of Durham Woods were scared out of their minds. "No words could ever tell you how frightening it was," said Kim Krajniak. "People were running out in their underwear. I felt like an animal running scared for my life."

7   People ran in all directions. Some headed for their cars only to burn their hands on the door handles. Some ran into the woods. Others dashed down the nearby railroad tracks. Those who could run fast pushed slower runners out of the way. Some stepped on people who had stumbled. Marlene Steinberg said it was "mass hysteria." She ran like everyone else. "We didn't know where we were going," she said, "but we kept going."

8   Barbara Williams didn't pay any attention to where she was headed. "Nobody had to give me directions," she said. "All I wanted to do was to get out of there as fast as I possibly could. And let me tell you, I ran like there was no tomorrow."

9 The blast shook Joy Anunwa out of bed. For a brief moment the light blinded her. Anunwa pinched herself. She wondered whether she had died and gone to heaven. Then she opened her apartment door. "The heat was like an oven. . . . It was right out of a disaster movie." She and her family headed for the woods.

10 The flames near the apartments began to spread. The intense heat melted the tires of cars. It blew out car windows and scorched the paint. When it reached the playground, the heat melted the swing sets. Luckily, a 20-foot dirt mound separated the apartment buildings from the fire. The mound slowed the fire's spread. It gave people about 10 minutes to get out. Those 10 minutes saved many lives.

11 When the fire did reach the apartment complex, it burned eight buildings to the ground. It damaged six others. Toni Strauch of the Red Cross said it was like an earthquake. "One day people have everything," she said. "The next day they are devastated."

12 In time, firefighters brought the blaze under control. Still, they feared the worst. The fire had totally wiped out 128 apartments. How many people would be found dead inside? Edison's mayor expected the death toll to be high. He couldn't believe it when he heard the truth. Only one person had

died. She was a 32-year-old woman who had suffered a heart attack. Many others were left with burns or injuries. But no one else perished. Incredibly, the fire itself didn't kill anyone. The mayor called it "a miracle of miracles."

13 Still, the terror didn't die out with the fire. "I try not to think about it," said Danielle Rhodes. But that was hard to do. The blast was imprinted on her mind. Four-year-old Michelle Varner also had trouble forgetting the explosion. In the nights that followed, she couldn't sleep. When her mother put her to bed, the little girl cried, "Mommy, when is the boom coming? I don't want to go to bed, the boom is coming."

14 Michelle's eight-year-old brother, Paris, had the same fear. "I don't want to go back [to my house]," he said. "I just want to move somewhere else. They said the pipeline had a hole in it. But even if they fix that, it could have another hole." Many Durham Woods residents shared his feelings.

15 But it is not easy to move away from gas pipelines. With its many branches, this one runs a total of about 26 thousand miles. Many of us live near this or similar pipelines. We just have to be more careful. Officials think the leak at Edison was caused by digging. Someone used the ground near the pipeline as a dump. Officials found 55-gallon drums buried there. They found

a crushed car buried on top of the pipeline. They also found car tires and steel rods buried there. In the process of burying these things, someone had dug into the ground. That could have weakened the pipe and caused the leak.

16 There are laws against such random digging. You can't just decide to dig a hole in the ground. All sorts of pipes and wires might be running below the ground. You don't know what you might hit. There are maps that show where the pipes and wires are. Clearly, someone in Edison didn't check. The result scared one person to death. And it left others with fears that won't go away.

If you have been timed while reading this article, enter your reading time below. Then turn to the Words-per-Minute Table on page 55 and look up your reading speed (words per minute). Enter your reading speed on the graph on page 56.

Reading Time: Lesson 1

_____ : _____
Minutes   *Seconds*

A | Finding the Main Idea

One statement below expresses the main idea of the article. One statement is too general, or too broad. The other statement explains only part of the article; it is too narrow. Label the statements using the following key:

M—Main Idea   **B—Too Broad**   **N—Too Narrow**

_____ 1. The destruction and chaos of a sudden, unexplained explosion can cause people to jump to false conclusions.

_____ 2. The gas pipeline under Edison, New Jersey, was 33 years old and was buried about seven feet deep.

_____ 3. In 1994 a huge gas explosion caused panic and confusion in the town of Edison, New Jersey.

_____ Score 15 points for a correct M answer.

_____ Score 5 points for each correct B or N answer.

_____ **Total Score:** Finding the Main Idea

B | Recalling Facts

How well do you remember the facts in the article? Put an X in the box next to the answer that correctly completes each statement about the article.

1. The pipeline carried natural gas to New Jersey from
☐ a. Florida.
☐ b. Texas.
☐ c. Alaska.

2. The Durham Woods Apartments were home to
☐ a. about 200 people.
☐ b. more than 1,500 people.
☐ c. more than 5,000 people.

3. This was *not* an effect of the intense heat:
☐ a. Car tires melted.
☐ b. Buildings burned down.
☐ c. Many people died.

4. Officials laid blame for the explosion on
☐ a. digging too close to the pipeline.
☐ b. impure gas in the pipeline.
☐ c. the use of poorly constructed pipes.

5. Near the pipeline, someone had buried
☐ a. nuclear waste.
☐ b. a crushed car and steel rods.
☐ c. a treasure chest.

Score 5 points for each correct answer.

_____ **Total Score:** Recalling Facts

C | Making Inferences

When you combine your own experience with information from a text to draw a conclusion that is not directly stated in that text, you are making an inference. Below are five statements that may or may not be inferences based on information in the article. Label the statements using the following key:

C—Correct Inference   F—Faulty Inference

_____ 1. Natural gas heating is more dangerous than other means of heating.

_____ 2. The Durham Woods Apartments were badly overcrowded.

_____ 3. The apartment complex welcomed residents with children.

_____ 4. Flames usually travel more slowly over mounded dirt than they do over flat, grassy ground.

_____ 5. Someone purposely tried to start an explosion by burying junk near the pipeline.

Score 5 points for each correct answer.

_____ **Total Score:** Making Inferences

D | Using Words Precisely

Each numbered sentence below contains an underlined word or phrase from the article. Following the sentence are three definitions. One definition is closest to the meaning of the underlined word. One definition is opposite or nearly opposite. Label those two definitions using the following key; do not label the remaining definition.

C—Closest   O—Opposite or Nearly Opposite

1. The heat from the blaze was a <u>searing</u> 1,000°F.

_____ a. burning

_____ b. cooling

_____ c. annoying

2. Marlene Steinberg said it was "mass <u>hysteria</u>."

_____ a. frenzy; panic

_____ b. talent

_____ c. peace and order

3. "One day people have everything," she said. "The next day they are <u>devastated</u>."

_____ a. organized

_____ b. relieved and thankful

_____ c. overwhelmed with sorrow and loss

4. But no one else <u>perished</u>.

_____ a. survived

_____ b. joined

_____ c. died

5. There are laws against such <u>random</u> digging.

_____ a. careful

_____ b. unplanned

_____ c. deep

_____ Score 3 points for each correct C answer.

_____ Score 2 points for each correct O answer.

_____ **Total Score:** Using Words Precisely

Enter the four total scores in the spaces below, and add them together to find your Reading Comprehension Score. Then record your score on the graph on page 57.

Score	Question Type	Lesson 1
_____	Finding the Main Idea	
_____	Recalling Facts	
_____	Making Inferences	
_____	Using Words Precisely	
_____	**Reading Comprehension Score**	

Author's Approach

Put an X in the box next to the correct answer.

1. What is the authors' purpose in writing "An Unexpected Explosion"?

☐ a.   to make readers worry about gas pipelines near their homes

☐ b.   to inform readers about a spectacular explosion and fire that surprised and frightened many people

☐ c.   to express disapproval of gas pipelines near homes

2. Which two of the following statements from the article best describe the gas pipeline before the explosion?

☐ a.   It blew a hole in the ground 120 feet wide and 60 feet deep.

☐ b.   It was like a good neighbor—quiet and helpful.

☐ c.   The natural gas pipeline made no noise.

3. From the statements below, choose those that you believe the authors would agree with.

☐ a.   It was amazing that only one person died in the disaster.

☐ b.   People should not dig at random near gas pipelines.

☐ c.   There should be no gas pipelines in the United States.

_____ Number of correct answers

Record your personal assessment of your work on the Critical Thinking Chart on page 58.

CRITICAL THINKING

19

Summarizing and Paraphrasing

Follow the directions provided for questions 1 and 3. Put an X in the box next to the correct answer for question 2.

1. Complete the following one-sentence summary of the article using the lettered phrases from the phrase bank below. Write the letters on the lines.

> **Phrase Bank:**
> a. what happened during the disaster
> b. a discussion about what caused the explosion
> c. a description of the pipeline before the explosion

The article about the explosion begins with _____, goes on

to explain _____, and ends with _____.

2. Choose the sentence that correctly restates the following sentence from the article "Luckily, a 20-foot dirt mound separated the apartment buildings from the fire."

☐ a. Luckily, the fire and a 20-foot dirt mound were separated by the apartments.

☐ b. It was lucky that the apartment buildings and the fire were near a 20-foot dirt mound.

☐ c. Fortunately, a 20-foot dirt mound stood between the fire and the apartments.

3. Look for the important ideas and events in paragraphs 10 and 11. Summarize those paragraphs in one or two sentences.

_____

_____

_____

_____

> _____ Number of correct answers
>
> Record your personal assessment of your work on the Critical Thinking Chart on page 58.

Critical Thinking

Put an X in the box next to the correct answer for questions 1, 2, and 5. Follow the directions provided for the other questions.

1. Which of the following statements from the article is an opinion rather than a fact?

☐ a. They found a crushed car buried on top of the pipeline.

☐ b. We just have to be more careful.

☐ c. With its many branches, this one [pipeline] runs a total of about 26 thousand miles.

2. From what eight-year-old Paris Varner said, you can predict that he will

☐ a. forget about the explosion very soon.

☐ b. remember this experience for years to come.

☐ c. persuade his little sister that there is nothing to fear.

3. Choose from the letters below to correctly complete the following statement. Write the letters on the lines.

In the article, _____ and _____ are alike.

a. the sound of a bomb going off

b. the sound of the Edison explosion

c. the sound of gas traveling through a pipeline

4. Choose from the letters below to correctly complete the following statement. Write the letters on the lines.

According to the article, _____ caused the pipeline to _____, and the effect was _____.

a. develop a leak

b. the pipeline exploded

c. careless digging near the pipeline

5. What did you have to do to answer question 3?

☐ a. find a comparison (how things are the same)

☐ b. find a definition (what something means)

☐ c. find a cause (why something happened)

_____ Number of correct answers

Record your personal assessment of your work on the Critical Thinking Chart on page 58.

Personal Response

What would you have done when the pipeline exploded if you had lived in the Durham Woods Apartments?

_____

_____

_____

_____

Self-Assessment

I was confused on question _____ in the _____ section because _____

_____

_____

_____

_____

The Fall of Saigon

Diem Do tried to be a good student. But it was hard. Each day he went to school. But each day his class got smaller.

"One day a couple of guys would be gone, and then a couple more. Then the teacher wouldn't show up," said 12-year-old Do. "Everyone was scared. They sensed that something tragic was about to happen."

2   It was April 1975. Do was going to school in Saigon, then the capital of South Vietnam. That country had been fighting North Vietnam for many years. Now the war was almost over. The United States had fought on the

Under attack by North Vietnamese forces, terrified South Vietnamese hurry to reach U.S. helicopters as they prepare to pull out of Saigon.

side of South Vietnam. But it was no use. A big army from North Vietnam was marching south. Its goal was to take over Saigon and end the war.

3   The Americans had gotten ready for the worst. They had plans to get themselves out of Saigon when the time came. By this time there weren't many Americans still there. Most had left years before. The problem was what to do with America's South Vietnamese friends. These people, too, hoped to get out before the enemy arrived. But there were far too many South Vietnamese. U.S. planes began to fly a few people out. But this was done slowly and quietly. Officials feared that if too many people thought the end was close, they might panic.

4   The army from the North, meanwhile, had its own schedule, and it was moving fast. By the last week of April, the army had Saigon surrounded. Each night, a college student named Nam Pham climbed to the roof of his home. He could see flashes of gunfire and bombs in the far distance. They kept getting closer and closer. Pham knew the South would soon lose. "It gave me kind of a weird feeling," he

said, "watching something you love so much lost a little bit every day."

5   On April 29, the North attacked Saigon itself. At four o'clock in the morning, they began to bomb the airport. When the Americans turned on their radios that morning, they heard "White Christmas." That song was a secret signal. It meant, "This is it. Everybody out!"

6   For the Vietnamese it was a different story. The blasts at the airport shook them out of their beds. Mass panic gripped the city. People dashed out of their homes, looking for a way—any way—to get out of town. Some people boarded boats and headed out to sea. The U.S. Navy had many large ships waiting offshore.

7   Loi Nguyen Vo was one of the lucky ones. She was living with her mother and six younger siblings. "We had to leave quickly with only the clothes on our back," she said. Taking charge, Vo went to look for a boat. Thousands of others lined the riverbank hoping for the same thing. Out of the mist, a patrol boat came by and picked up Vo and her family. "I still don't know why we were picked.

We were very lucky," said Vo many years later.

8　　Many Vietnamese rushed to the U.S. embassy. The Americans had been their friends. Surely America would help them now. But what could the Americans do? There were thousands of people swarming around the embassy gates. They all wanted to flee. But time was running out. The North was closing in. Frank Snepp, an American, tried to restore order. "Don't worry," he told the mob. "We won't leave you!" Snepp was lying. There was no way to evacuate this many people in just a few hours. He later said the scene was like a "vision out of a nightmare."

9　　The bombing closed the airport. So no one could fly out from there. Driving out of town wasn't possible either. The army of the North had all the roads blocked. Other than by boat, the only way out was by helicopter. American pilots flew helicopters back and forth from the ships at sea to Saigon. They had to land on the roof of the embassy. It was the only safe flat place they could find. The pilots took as many Vietnamese as they could. But far more had to be left behind. "These people were desperate to escape," said one pilot. "But we could only hold so many."

10　　Tini Tran was only three years old at the time. Many years later she could still recall what it was like. Her parents brought her to the embassy gates. But they soon lost her in the crowd. Luckily Tran's uncle found her. "He hoisted me up as he shoved his way through the crowd," recalled Tran. "Afraid I would become trampled in the crush, my uncle handed me into the arms of an American." Luckily the rest of her family also made it out.

11　　If the fall of Saigon had any heroes, they were the helicopter pilots. Time after time they risked their lives. Darrell Browning had never flown in combat. Now he faced many dangers. He worried about being shot down. The army of the North could do it. So, too, could a soldier from the South. Some of these soldiers were angry at the United States for leaving them alone to face the enemy. Also, Browning flew late into the night with his lights out. With choppers flying all over the place, he might have hit one in midair. Luckily, nothing like that happened.

12　　Each time Browning landed on the roof, people fought each other for a seat. He helped as many as he could. His chopper was built to carry 24 people. Still, he let 36 get on board. He figured the Vietnamese people tended to be small, so they weighed less. Even so, he worried he couldn't take off with all the extra weight. Somehow, he did. By midnight, he had made five round trips between his ship and the roof.

13　　Then he was told to stop. It was over. The chopper pilots were worn out. One exhausted pilot missed his ship and crashed into the sea. The officer in charge worried that other pilots would also make tragic mistakes.

14　　The next day, April 30, the army of the North captured Saigon. The war was over. In all, about 50,000 South Vietnamese escaped. Some were on the deck of Darrell Browning's ship. Many were the people he had helped to save the night before. "There were about a thousand of them," he said. "They had lost everything. They had no idea where they were going and they were tired. But they were orderly and thankful. They came up and thanked us." For them, at least, the nightmare was over.

If you have been timed while reading this article, enter your reading time below. Then turn to the Words-per-Minute Table on page 55 and look up your reading speed (words per minute). Enter your reading speed on the graph on page 56.

Reading Time: Lesson 2

――――― : ―――――
Minutes　　　Seconds

A | Finding the Main Idea

One statement below expresses the main idea of the article. One statement is too general, or too broad. The other statement explains only part of the article; it is too narrow. Label the statements using the following key:

M—Main Idea   **B—Too Broad**   **N—Too Narrow**

_____ 1. The end of a war almost always brings panic and hardship to the losers.

_____ 2. Just before the city of Saigon was captured at the end of the war in Vietnam, people desperately tried to escape. During the final hours, people panicked and fought each other in order to board U.S. helicopters.

_____ 3. Just before the fall of Saigon, American helicopter pilots repeatedly landed on the roof of the American embassy to pick up passengers.

_____ Score 15 points for a correct M answer.

_____ Score 5 points for each correct B or N answer.

_____ **Total Score:** Finding the Main Idea

B | Recalling Facts

How well do you remember the facts in the article? Put an X in the box next to the answer that correctly completes each statement about the article.

1. The North Vietnamese army attacked Saigon on
☐ a. April 29, 1975.
☐ b. July 29, 1965.
☐ c. December 6, 1980.

2. Americans living in Saigon knew it was time to leave when they heard
☐ a. "Here Comes Peter Cottontail."
☐ b. "We Gotta Get Out of This Place."
☐ c. "White Christmas."

3. People couldn't leave Saigon by plane because
☐ a. all the pilots had already evacuated.
☐ b. the North Vietnamese were bombing the airport.
☐ c. all the planes had been destroyed.

4. The only ways to get out of Saigon at this time were
☐ a. by helicopter and by boat.
☐ b. by private car and by private airplane.
☐ c. by army truck and by tank.

5. U.S. Army officials finally stopped the helicopter evacuation after
☐ a. the North Vietnamese army canceled their attack.
☐ b. everyone who wanted to leave had been evacuated.
☐ c. one tired pilot crashed into the sea.

_____ Score 5 points for each correct answer.

_____ **Total Score:** Recalling Facts

C | Making Inferences

When you combine your own experience with information from a text to draw a conclusion that is not directly stated in that text, you are making an inference. Below are five statements that may or may not be inferences based on information in the article. Label the statements using the following key:

C—Correct Inference   **F—Faulty Inference**

_____ 1. The fall of Saigon came as a surprise to the Americans living there.

_____ 2. Americans in Saigon listened to their radios a great deal during April 1975.

_____ 3. South Vietnamese people who had been friendly with Americans feared the North Vietnamese.

_____ 4. Though desperate to escape, people trying to board the helicopters politely allowed those who were injured, very young, or very old to board first.

_____ 5. It is dangerous to fly a helicopter in the dark without lights.

Score 5 points for each correct answer.

_____ **Total Score:** Making Inferences

D | Using Words Precisely

Each numbered sentence below contains an underlined word or phrase from the article. Following the sentence are three definitions. One definition is closest to the meaning of the underlined word. One definition is opposite or nearly opposite. Label those two definitions using the following key; do not label the remaining definition.

C—Closest   **O—Opposite or Nearly Opposite**

1. They all wanted to <u>flee</u>.

_____ a. come back

_____ b. run away; escape

_____ c. learn

2. Many years later she could still <u>recall</u> what it was like.

_____ a. remember

_____ b. describe

_____ c. forget

3. "He <u>hoisted</u> me up as he shoved his way through the crowd," recalled Tran.

_____ a. tied

_____ b. dropped

_____ c. lifted

4. Darrell Browning had never flown in <u>combat</u>.

_____ a. battle

_____ b. helicopters

_____ c. peacetime

5. The next day, April 30, the army of the North <u>captured</u> Saigon.

_____ a. gave up

_____ b. took over

_____ c. fired upon

_____ Score 3 points for each correct C answer.

_____ Score 2 points for each correct O answer.

_____ **Total Score:** Using Words Precisely

Enter the four total scores in the spaces below, and add them together to find your Reading Comprehension Score. Then record your score on the graph on page 57.

Score	Question Type	Lesson 2
_____	Finding the Main Idea	
_____	Recalling Facts	
_____	Making Inferences	
_____	Using Words Precisely	
_____	**Reading Comprehension Score**	

Author's Approach

Put an X in the box next to the correct answer.

1. Judging by statements from the article "The Fall of Saigon," you can conclude that the authors want the reader to think that
   ☐ a. Americans didn't really care about the South Vietnamese whom they left behind.
   ☐ b. Americans wanted to help the South Vietnamese, but they couldn't.
   ☐ c. Americans were angry with the South Vietnamese people.

2. Choose the statement below that best describes the authors' position in paragraph 11.
   ☐ a. The helicopter pilots were heroes who risked their lives.
   ☐ b. The helicopter pilots did not know how to fly in a safe way.
   ☐ c. South Vietnamese soldiers had no reason to be angry with the United States.

3. The authors probably wrote this article to
   ☐ a. criticize the Americans in Saigon.
   ☐ b. describe a situation in which desperate people panicked.
   ☐ c. explain the reasons for the war in Vietnam.

4. The authors tell this story mainly by
   ☐ a. using their imagination and creativity.
   ☐ b. comparing different topics.
   ☐ c. telling about events in the order they happened.

_____ Number of correct answers

Record your personal assessment of your work on the Critical Thinking Chart on page 58.

Summarizing and Paraphrasing

Follow the directions provided for questions 1 and 2. Put an X in the box next to the correct answer for question 3.

1. Complete the following one-sentence summary of the article using the lettered phrases from the phrase bank below. Write the letters on the lines.

Phrase Bank

a. a description of successful escapees aboard a U.S. ship

b. the events that came before the fall of Saigon

c. how people tried to escape Saigon after the North Vietnamese attacked

---

The article "The Fall of Saigon" begins with _____, goes on

to explain _____, and ends with _____.

2. Reread paragraph 8 in the article. Below, write a summary of the paragraph in no more than 25 words.

_____

_____

_____

_____

Reread your summary and decide whether it covers the important ideas in the paragraph. Next, decide how to shorten the summary to 15 words or less without leaving out any essential information. Write this summary below.

_____

_____

_____

3. Read the statement below from the article. Then read the paraphrase of that statement. Choose the reason that best tells why the paraphrase does not say the same thing as the statement.

Statement: Darrell Browning let 36 people board his helicopter, even though it was built to hold only 24.

Paraphrase: Although Darrell Browning's helicopter could hold 36 people, he allowed only 24 on board.

☐ a. Paraphrase says too much.

☐ b. Paraphrase doesn't say enough.

☐ c. Paraphrase doesn't agree with the statement.

_____ Number of correct answers

Record your personal assessment of your work on the Critical Thinking Chart on page 58.

Critical Thinking

Follow the directions provided for questions 1, 2, and 3. Put an X in the box next to the correct answer for question 4.

1. For each statement below, write *O* if it expresses an opinion or write *F* if it expresses a fact.

_____ a. Americans should not have left their friends to face the enemy alone.

_____ b. On April 30 the North Vietnamese captured Saigon.

_____ c. U.S. helicopters landed on the embassy roof, picked up passengers, and took them to ships waiting offshore.

2. Choose from the letters below to correctly complete the following statement. Write the letters on the lines.

On the positive side, _____, but on the negative side

_____.

a. about 50,000 people escaped Saigon

b. many frightened people were left in Saigon

c. many people hoped that the Americans could help them escape

3. Reread paragraph 11. Then choose from the letters below to correctly complete the following statement. Write the letters on the lines.

According to paragraph 11, _____ because _____.

a. Darrell Browning had never flown in combat

b. some South Vietnamese soldiers were angry at the United States.

c. the soldiers felt the Americans were deserting them

4. What did you have to do to answer question 3?

☐ a. find an opinion (what someone thinks about something)

☐ b. find a contrast (how things are different)

☐ c. find a cause (why something happened)

_____ Number of correct answers

Record your personal assessment of your work on the Critical Thinking Chart on page 58.

Personal Response

Describe a time when you were afraid of being left behind or forgotten. Tell how you felt.

_____

_____

_____

_____

Self-Assessment

Which concepts or ideas from the article were difficult to understand?

_____

_____

_____

Which were easy?

_____

_____

_____

Firetrap!

Julio Gonzalez was mad—really mad. First, he had lost his job. Now he was broke. He had to hustle spare change from strangers on the streets of New York City. And to top it all off, his girlfriend, Lydia Feliciano, had just said she did not want to see him anymore.

2   Gonzalez hoped to win Lydia back. On March 24, 1990, he went to see her at the Happy Land Club in the Bronx. Lydia worked there taking tickets and checking coats. But things didn't go the way Gonzalez had planned. The

The Happy Land Club did not live up to its name in the early morning hours of March 25, 1990. The tiny club had been filled with fun-seekers, mostly Honduran immigrants. All but five of the 92 people inside died in a fire set by the angry boyfriend of a club employee.

two began to argue. "Leave me alone! Leave me alone!" Lydia cried.

3   Gonzalez, who had been drinking, wasn't thinking clearly. He became furious. He started swearing at her. At that point, the club bouncer told him to leave. "I will be back," Gonzalez threatened. "I will shut this place down."

4   Gonzalez kept his dire threat. Around three o'clock the next morning, he returned to the club. He carried with him a plastic can filled with gasoline. He had paid a dollar for it at a local gas station. Gonzalez splashed the gasoline around the club's front door. Then he tossed a lighted match on the gas. As the flames climbed up the door, Gonzalez just stood there and watched. Then he walked down the street and back to his room.

5   Inside the club were dozens of young people. Most were immigrants from Honduras. They had packed the place, coming to dance and have a good time. They were listening to the music they loved—salsa, reggae, and calypso. One lucky man had left at one o'clock. The club was too crowded for him. "You could barely move," he later

said. "I had a feeling something could go wrong."

6   Even without Julio Gonzalez, there were lots of things that could have gone wrong at Happy Land. The club was unsafe. The city had ordered it closed 16 months earlier. The small, two-story club was a firetrap. It had no fire exits or emergency lights. It had no sprinkler system. It didn't have a fire alarm.

7   Lots of people knew about the fire hazards. A man named Jerome Ford explained how he had tried to warn his family. He had spoken to his niece, his cousin, and his wife's three brothers. "I told them not to go," he said. "But kids are kids. I knew it was dangerous."

8   The dangers meant nothing to Elias Colon, the club's owner. To him, the Happy Land Club was a great moneymaker. So he kept the place open. Although the city had told him to close it, officials did nothing to enforce the order. One city worker explained how hard it was to get such places closed down. "You shut them down one day, and they reopen the next," he said.

9   New York City had hundreds of these clubs. They were all illegal. None had the city licenses they needed. Few, if any, met the city's fire code. But these "social clubs" seemed to fill a void in people's lives. They gave immigrants a place to relax with their own people. They were an old tradition in New York City.

10   The Happy Land Club was not an exception. Most of the regulars were looking for a club of their own. They had settled on Happy Land. The prices were low, and the music was loud. It even felt a bit like home. "It was great," said one man. "You could dance, you could get a drink. It was beautiful."

11   But there was nothing beautiful about it in the early morning of March 25, 1990. The blaze Gonzalez had set spread quickly. Thick black smoke billowed up inside the club. It soon reached the second-story dance floor, where all the people were. Not only did this area lack fire exits, it also lacked windows. The people up here were trapped. Some ran to the stairs, hoping to get down to the first floor. But the fire stopped most of them. A few did make it down. But even then, there was no way out. There were two small windows on the ground floor. But both were blocked. One had bars, and the other held an air conditioner.

12   Firefighters got to the scene as fast as they could. They heard no screams. They saw no one fleeing from the building. The people trapped inside were already dead. Sixty-eight bodies were found on the second floor. Nineteen more were discovered on the ground level. Among the dead was Happy Land owner Elias Colon.

13   It was the smoke, not the fire, that killed most people. The smoke suffocated them before they could react. Some died so fast they still had their drinks in their hands; some still had their legs wrapped around a bar stool. Many had thrown themselves into corners, hoping the smoke wouldn't reach that far.

14   Firefighter Richard Harden helped put out the fire. Then he helped remove the bodies. The tale of terror still showed on the victims' faces. "Some looked horrified," he said. "Some looked like they were in shock. There were some people holding hands. Some people had torn their clothes off in their panic to get out."

15   The Happy Land fire was the worst fire New York City had seen in a long time. [The worst ever had occurred exactly 79 years earlier. On March 25, 1911, the Triangle Shirtwaist factory had caught fire. That blaze killed 146 women. They, too, were mostly immigrants.]

16   Five people made it out of Happy Land alive. These five found a seldom-used door on the first floor. Outside, a gate blocked their escape. They managed to force it open and get away. One of the five was Julio Gonzalez's ex-girlfriend, Lydia Feliciano.

17   Meanwhile, back in his room, Gonzalez went to bed. The police arrested him there later in the day. Gonzalez quickly admitted his guilt. When he realized what he had done, he began to cry. "I got angry," he said. "The devil got into me." His tears may have been sincere. But they couldn't bring back the 87 people who died in the Happy Land Club.

If you have been timed while reading this article, enter your reading time below. Then turn to the Words-per-Minute Table on page 55 and look up your reading speed (words per minute). Enter your reading speed on the graph on page 56.

Reading Time: Lesson 3

_____ : _____
Minutes   *Seconds*

A Finding the Main Idea

One statement below expresses the main idea of the article. One statement is too general, or too broad. The other statement explains only part of the article; it is too narrow. Label the statements using the following key:

M—Main Idea   **B—Too Broad**   **N—Too Narrow**

_____ 1. The worst fire in New York City in recent years occurred on March 25, 1990, exactly 79 years after the worst fire in the city's history.

_____ 2. It is necessary that cities make and enforce laws that require fire exits, sprinkler systems, and fire-resistant material in public buildings.

_____ 3. Eighty-seven people packed into an unsafe and illegal dance club in New York City died within minutes after a man started a fire at the club.

_____ Score 15 points for a correct M answer.

_____ Score 5 points for each correct B or N answer.

_____ **Total Score:** Finding the Main Idea

B Recalling Facts

How well do you remember the facts in the article? Put an X in the box next to the answer that correctly completes each statement about the article.

1. Because his girlfriend no longer wanted him, Julio Gonzalez
   □ a. threatened her boss with fire.
   □ b. killed the woman in a fire.
   □ c. set fire to the club where she worked.

2. After Gonzalez started the fire, he
   □ a. went home to bed.
   □ b. ran to call the fire department.
   □ c. locked the door to keep people from escaping from the building.

3. Most of the people at the Happy Land Club were
   □ a. from Honduras.
   □ b. out of a job.
   □ c. rich and famous.

4. The club's owner, Elias Colon,
   □ a. had obeyed city laws carefully.
   □ b. had ignored orders to make his club safe.
   □ c. was interested more in safety than in profit.

5. Most of the customers inside the club
   □ a. died from smoke in minutes.
   □ b. ran out a little-used door.
   □ c. were still screaming when firefighters arrived.

Score 5 points for each correct answer.

_____ **Total Score:** Recalling Facts

C │ Making Inferences

When you combine your own experience with information from a text to draw a conclusion that is not directly stated in that text, you are making an inference. Below are five statements that may or may not be inferences based on information in the article. Label the statements using the following key:

C—Correct Inference   **F—Faulty Inference**

_____ 1. Usually, a disaster caused by humans is the result of an elaborate plan to create panic.

_____ 2. Passing laws about safety makes everyone safer.

_____ 3. Whenever you are in a crowded area, it's a good idea to find at least two different ways out.

_____ 4. March 25 is an unlucky day for New Yorkers.

_____ 5. Only safety experts could recognize the problems that made the Happy Land Club dangerous.

Score 5 points for each correct answer.

_____ **Total Score:** Making Inferences

D │ Using Words Precisely

Each numbered sentence below contains an underlined word or phrase from the article. Following the sentence are three definitions. One definition is closest to the meaning of the underlined word. One definition is opposite or nearly opposite. Label those two definitions using the following key; do not label the remaining definition.

C—Closest   **O—Opposite or Nearly Opposite**

1. Gonzalez kept his <u>dire</u> threat.

_____ a. terrible; horrible

_____ b. cheerful

_____ c. thoughtless

2. Inside the club were dozens of young people. Most were <u>immigrants</u> from Honduras.

_____ a. people who were born in another country

_____ b. people who come into a new country

_____ c. factory workers

3. The Happy Land Club was not an <u>exception</u>.

_____ a. one of the oldest of its kind

_____ b. the usual thing

_____ c. a special case

4. Not only did this area <u>lack</u> fire exits, it also lacked windows.

_____ a. have in great numbers

_____ b. charge for

_____ c. to be without

5. His tears may have been <u>sincere</u>.

_____ a. in great quantity

_____ b. honest; true

_____ c. false

_____ Score 3 points for each correct C answer.

_____ Score 2 points for each correct O answer.

_____ **Total Score:** Using Words Precisely

Enter the four total scores in the spaces below, and add them together to find your Reading Comprehension Score. Then record your score on the graph on page 57.

Score	Question Type	Lesson 3
_____	Finding the Main Idea	
_____	Recalling Facts	
_____	Making Inferences	
_____	Using Words Precisely	
_____	**Reading Comprehension Score**	

Author's Approach

Put an X in the box next to the correct answer.

1. What do the authors mean by the statement "As the flames climbed up the door, Gonzalez just stood there and watched"?

☐ a. Gonzalez purposely did not stop the spread of the fire.

☐ b. Gonzalez was so terrified that he was frozen to the spot.

☐ c. Although he wanted to help, Gonzalez couldn't figure out what to do next.

2. The main purpose of the first paragraph is to

☐ a. make readers feel sorry for Gonzalez.

☐ b. describe life in New York City.

☐ c. explain why Gonzalez was angry.

3. Judging by statements from the article "Firetrap!" you can conclude that the authors want the reader to think that

☐ a. the tragedy could have been prevented if the club had followed fire safety rules.

☐ b. Gonzalez never meant to hurt anyone.

☐ c. there is really no one to blame for the tragedy.

4. Choose the statement below that best describes the authors' position in paragraph 17.

☐ a. Gonzalez was really a nice man who just made a mistake.

☐ b. Gonzalez may have been sorry, but his sorrow was useless after his victims were already dead.

☐ c. When you get angry, you can't be blamed for committing violent crimes.

_____ Number of correct answers

Record your personal assessment of your work on the Critical Thinking Chart on page 58.

Summarizing and Paraphrasing

Put an X in the box next to the correct answer for questions 1 and 3. Follow the directions provided for question 2.

1. Below are summaries of the article. Choose the summary that says all the most important things about the article but in the fewest words.

   ☐ a. When fire broke out in the Happy Land Club, 87 young people died. Only five people escaped the blaze and its terrible smoke. Luckily, they found a seldom-used door on the first floor.

   ☐ b. Recent immigrants from Honduras enjoyed music and fun at the Happy Land Club until fire broke out in 1990.

   ☐ c. Angry with his girlfriend, Julio Gonzalez set a fire at the Happy Land Club in New York City. Because the club's owner hadn't followed fire safety rules, 87 people died in the blaze.

2. Reread paragraph 3 in the article. Below, write a summary of the paragraph in no more than 25 words.

   _____

   _____

   _____

   _____

   Reread your summary and decide whether it covers the important ideas in the paragraph. Next, decide how to shorten the summary to 15 words or less without leaving out any essential information. Write this summary below.

   _____

   _____

   _____

3. Choose the best one-sentence paraphrase for the following sentence from the article "The dangers meant nothing to Elias Colon, the club's owner."

   ☐ a. Elias Colon, the club's owner, couldn't understand how his club could be dangerous.

   ☐ b. The club's owner, Elias Colon, didn't care that his club was dangerous.

   ☐ c. Elias Colon, the club's owner, didn't understand the word *dangers*.

   _____ Number of correct answers

   Record your personal assessment of your work on the Critical Thinking Chart on page 58.

Critical Thinking

Follow the directions provided for questions 1, 2, and 3. Put an X in the box next to the correct answer for question 4.

1. For each statement below, write *O* if it expresses an opinion or write *F* if it expresses a fact.

   _____ a. When firefighters arrived they saw no one running away from the building.

   _____ b. The Happy Land Club should not have been allowed to operate without proper safety precautions.

   _____ c. One of the people to escape the fire was Gonzalez's ex-girlfriend.

2. Using what is told about the Triangle Shirtwaist factory fire and what is told about the Happy Land tragedy in the article, name three ways the Happy Land tragedy is similar to and three ways the Happy Land tragedy is different from the Triangle Shirtwaist factory fire. Cite the paragraph number(s) where you found details in the article to support your conclusions.

Similarities

_____

_____

_____

Differences

_____

_____

_____

3. Reread paragraph 12. Then choose from the letters below to correctly complete the following statement. Write the letters on the lines.

According to paragraph 12, _____ because _____.

a. firefighters reached the blaze as soon as they could

b. firefighters didn't hear any screams coming from the Happy Land Club

c. all the people inside were dead

4. What did you have to do to answer question 3?

☐ a. find an opinion (what someone thinks about something)

☐ b. find a list (a number of things)

☐ c. find a cause (why something happened)

_____ Number of correct answers

Record your personal assessment of your work on the Critical Thinking Chart on page 58.

Personal Response

A question I would like answered by Julio Gonzalez is _____

_____

_____

Self-Assessment

One of the things I did best when reading this article was _____

_____

_____

I believe I did this well because _____

_____

_____

A Deadly Plunge

Rescue teams drag the remains of the Sunset Limited *out of the Big Bayou Canot in Alabama. The train had been carrying 210 sleeping passengers through a foggy night when disaster suddenly struck.*

A thick fog had moved in. Willie Odom could barely see through the gloomy darkness. Odom was at the wheel of the tugboat *Mauvilla*. He was pushing a string of six barges up the Mobile River. At least, he thought he was on the Mobile River. Odom did not realize it, but he had taken a wrong turn. The *Mauvilla* was now in Big Bayou Canot. Tugs weren't supposed to be in this small Alabama river. The barges they pushed were too large for Big Bayou.

2   As Odom moved upstream, he felt a sudden bump. "It wasn't [a] real

hard bump," he later said. "[But] it wasn't a real soft bump." Odom figured one of the barges might have hit some small log or piece of debris. But it was worse than that—much worse. One of the barges had hit a low-hanging railroad bridge. The bridge was knocked 70 feet out of alignment. That meant the train tracks now ran straight into the murky river. In just a couple of minutes, a train would come speeding down these very tracks.

3   It was September 22, 1993. At 2:53 A.M., a train did approach the bridge. It was an Amtrak train called the *Sunset Limited*. It was carrying 210 people. The train was zipping along at 70 miles per hour. Without warning, it hit the broken tracks. Three engines and four of the train's cars plunged off the bridge and burst into flames. The four remaining cars derailed and jammed into each other on the tracks above. One car was left hanging, half in the water, half in the air.

4   The crash sent everyone sprawling. Conductor Gary Lee Farmer was at the back of the train. He was with crew member Dwight Thompson. Farmer later talked about the crash.

"It was like flying into the side of a mountain," he said. "There was a horrendous impact. I was sliding down the aisle on my stomach. Mr. Thompson came sailing over my head."

5   Farmer grabbed his radio. He sent out a distress call. Then he began working his way to the front of the train. He wanted to check out the damage. He wanted to see if there was anything he could do to help.

6   In the cars still on the bridge, Farmer said, "It was sheer chaos. People were all over the place." As he neared the front cars, he saw that a diesel-fuel fire had broken out on the surface of the water. It threatened to spread to the rest of the train. Meanwhile, the car that was dangling in the air was beginning to sink down. Some people were in the water. They were screaming, splashing. One elderly woman was being carried downstream.

7   With no thought for his own safety, Farmer jumped into the oily water. He rescued the woman. Then he tried to save those still trapped in the sinking car. But he couldn't get the car door open. The thought of people dying on

the other side of that door upset him badly. "That will haunt me for the rest of my life," he said.

8   Farmer was one hero. There were others. Those who were not badly hurt did their best to help. Charlie Jones, a waiter on the train, had been sleeping. The crash caused the bunk above him to break off the wall. It fell on top of Jones. "Somehow, I was able to get out from under [the bunk]," he said.

9   But then he heard a voice calling out from the next compartment. "I can't get out! My door won't open! I can't get out! Please help me, I'm beginning to burn." It was one of Jones's friends. Jones struggled to get the door open, but it was just not possible. The door wouldn't budge; it was jammed shut. "I tried hard to get him out," said Jones later. "It was no use." Finally, the smoke became too intense. Despite his brave effort, Jones had to leave his friend behind.

10   Michael Dopheide had more success. The 26-year-old Dopheide was in the car that ended up half in the water. He had been asleep when the train ran off the bridge. The impact hurled him to the floor. Dopheide

stumbled to his feet. It was dark. Earlier, he had stashed his glasses in his boots, and he didn't have time to look for them. A wooden piling had broken one of the windows. Muddy water was rushing into the car. Already the water was up to his waist. Dopheide knew he had to act quickly. He heard a woman shouting, "Oh God, we're all gonna die!"

11   Somehow Dopheide found the emergency exit. With help from some other people, he removed the window from the exit door. Then he jumped into the water. He turned his attention to saving others. There was no time to waste. Anyone left in the car would soon drown.

12   From the exit door, it was a six-foot drop to the water. Some people were afraid to jump that far. Some were afraid of the snakes and alligators that were known to live in the bayou. And some did not want to jump because they could not swim. Yet, one after another, Dopheide coaxed people into

the water. Donnie Hughes was one of those people. She couldn't swim. As she perched in the metal frame of the exit door, she froze. "Then I looked below and saw [Dopheide]. He was saying, 'It's OK. I'm here, come on, I've got ya.'" Hughes did jump, and Dopheide pulled her to safety. In all, he saved more than 30 lives.

13   Back on the *Mauvilla*, Willie Odom realized what had happened. He turned his tug around and came to help. But the heat and flames kept him from getting too close. Still, Odom lowered two small boats and some life jackets into the water. Dopheide lifted several people up to him. One was a two-year-old girl. Another was an elderly lady. A third was a crippled child. Odom knew his wrong turn had caused this. All he could say to these people was, "I'm sorry."

14   It took hours to rescue all the survivors. The bridge was in a remote area. The nearest road was six miles away. Helicopters had to wait until

dawn for the fog to clear. At long last, help did arrive. But it was too late for 47 people. The fog, the fire—and human error—had combined to create the worst accident in the history of Amtrak.

If you have been timed while reading this article, enter your reading time below. Then turn to the Words-per-Minute Table on page 55 and look up your reading speed (words per minute). Enter your reading speed on the graph on page 56.

Reading Time: Lesson 4

_____ : _____
Minutes   Seconds

A | Finding the Main Idea

One statement below expresses the main idea of the article. One statement is too general, or too broad. The other statement explains only part of the article; it is too narrow. Label the statements using the following key:

M—Main Idea　　　**B—Too Broad**　　　**N—Too Narrow**

_____ 1. The worst accident in the history of the Amtrak rail line occurred on a bridge over a small Alabama river, due to fog and human error.

_____ 2. After a train plunged off a bridge struck by a barge, heroic passengers and rescuers combined to save most people on board from fire and drowning.

_____ 3. Michael Dopheide saved more than 30 people trapped in a railroad car that was knocked partway off a bridge.

_____ Score 15 points for a correct M answer.

_____ Score 5 points for each correct B or N answer.

_____ **Total Score:** Finding the Main Idea

B | Recalling Facts

How well do you remember the facts in the article? Put an X in the box next to the answer that correctly completes each statement about the article.

1. The bridge was knocked out of alignment by
   - ☐ a. the tugboat *Mauvilla*.
   - ☐ b. one of six barges pushed by a tugboat.
   - ☐ c. barges carried away by floodwater.

2. The train that crashed on the bridge carried
   - ☐ a. 47 people.
   - ☐ b. 70 people.
   - ☐ c. 210 people.

3. The engines and first four cars of the train
   - ☐ a. plunged off the bridge and burst into flames.
   - ☐ b. jammed into each other before falling.
   - ☐ c. fell into the river and floated away.

4. Both a conductor and a waiter tried to save people but were not able to
   - ☐ a. get frantic people to follow directions.
   - ☐ b. open doors that were jammed shut.
   - ☐ c. swim.

5. People in the car dangling between the bridge and the river saved themselves by
   - ☐ a. remaining motionless until rescuers arrived.
   - ☐ b. crawling up the car and back to the bridge.
   - ☐ c. jumping into the water.

Score 5 points for each correct answer.

_____ **Total Score:** Recalling Facts

41

C | Making Inferences

When you combine your own experience with information from a text to draw a conclusion that is not directly stated in that text, you are making an inference. Below are five statements that may or may not be inferences based on information in the article. Label the statements using the following key:

C—Correct Inference   **F—Faulty Inference**

_____ 1. There is no way to automatically inform train engineers when something damages track in front of their trains.

_____ 2. Barges are never allowed to pass under railway bridges.

_____ 3. Trains, barges, and other vehicles should not be allowed to travel in fog.

_____ 4. Improvements are needed in the design of emergency exits of railroad passenger cars.

_____ 5. The pilot of the tugboat involved in this wreck was unfit for his job.

Score 5 points for each correct answer.

_____ **Total Score:** Making Inferences

D | Using Words Precisely

Each numbered sentence below contains an underlined word or phrase from the article. Following the sentence are three definitions. One definition is closest to the meaning of the underlined word. One definition is opposite or nearly opposite. Label those two definitions using the following key; do not label the remaining definition.

C—Closest   **O—Opposite or Nearly Opposite**

1. The bridge was knocked 70 feet out of <u>alignment.</u>

_____ a. disorder

_____ b. consideration

_____ c. arrangement in a straight line

2. "It was like flying into the side of a mountain," he said. "There was a horrendous <u>impact.</u>"

_____ a. noise

_____ b. separation

_____ c. violent contact

3. Meanwhile, the car that was <u>dangling</u> in the air was beginning to sink down.

_____ a. hanging

_____ b. attached solidly

_____ c. falling apart

4. Yet, one after another, Dopheide <u>coaxed</u> people into the water.

_____ a. persuaded; urged

_____ b. greeted

_____ c. discouraged

5. As she perched in the metal frame of the exit door, she <u>froze</u>.

_____ a. moved easily

_____ b. became unable to move

_____ c. became chilled

_____ Score 3 points for each correct C answer.

_____ Score 2 points for each correct O answer.

_____ **Total Score:** Using Words Precisely

Enter the four total scores in the spaces below, and add them together to find your Reading Comprehension Score. Then record your score on the graph on page 57.

Score	Question Type	Lesson 4
_____	Finding the Main Idea	
_____	Recalling Facts	
_____	Making Inferences	
_____	Using Words Precisely	
_____	**Reading Comprehension Score**	

Author's Approach

Put an X in the box next to the correct answer.

1. The main purpose of the first paragraph is to

☐ a. describe the tugboat *Mauvilla*.

☐ b. explain the problem the tugboat had gotten into.

☐ c. tell where tugboats should and should not go on Alabama waterways.

2. What do the authors imply by saying "The fog, the fire—and human error—had combined to create the worst accident in the history of Amtrak"?

☐ a. The engineers who put the railroad track so low were mostly to blame for this accident.

☐ b. It was the fault of the passengers on the train that so many people died in the accident.

☐ c. Willie Odom, the captain of the tugboat, was partially to blame for this accident.

3. The authors probably wrote this article to

☐ a. stress the heroic way some people acted during the crisis.

☐ b. show how dangerous fog can be.

☐ c. inform readers about a terrible accident that caused panic.

4. The authors tell this story mainly by

☐ a. describing events in the order they happened.

☐ b. comparing different topics.

☐ c. using their imagination and creativity.

_____ Number of correct answers

Record your personal assessment of your work on the Critical Thinking Chart on page 58.

Summarizing and Paraphrasing

Follow the directions provided for question 1. Put an X in the box next to the correct answer for question 2.

1. Look for the important ideas and events in paragraphs 11 and 12. Summarize those paragraphs in one or two sentences.

_____

_____

_____

_____

2. Read the statement from the article below. Then read the paraphrase of that statement. Choose the reason that best tells why the paraphrase does not say the same thing as the statement.

   Statement: Of the eight cars in the train, four fell off the bridge and into the water, and four more cars derailed.

   Paraphrase: Four train cars fell into the water and four were derailed; one car dangled half in the water.

   ☐ a. Paraphrase says too much.

   ☐ b. Paraphrase doesn't say enough.

   ☐ c. Paraphrase doesn't agree with the statement.

   _____ Number of correct answers

   Record your personal assessment of your work on the Critical Thinking Chart on page 58.

Critical Thinking

Follow the directions provided for questions 1, 2, and 5. Put an X in the box next to the correct answer for the other questions.

1. For each statement below, write *O* if it expresses an opinion or write *F* if it expresses a fact.

   _____ a. When they are in danger, people lose their common sense.

   _____ b. Michael Dopheide is responsible for saving more than 30 lives.

   _____ c. People often show their best qualities when faced with a crisis.

2. Choose from the letters below to correctly complete the following statement. Write the letters on the lines.

   In the article, _____ and _____ are different.

   a. Gary Farmer's success in saving the lives of passengers in a sinking car

   b. Charlie Jones's success in saving his friend's life

   c. Michael Dopheide's success in saving passengers' lives

3. What was the cause of Willie Odom's wrong turn?

   ☐ a. Willie Odom was not paying close attention to his job.

   ☐ b. A thick fog made it impossible to see the correct way to go.

   ☐ c. A bad storm had knocked out the lights on shore that should have shown the way.

4. How is "A Deadly Plunge" related to the theme of *Total Panic*?

☐ a. Passengers were terrified and were running around wildly in their effort to survive.

☐ b. Many deaths occurred as a result of the accident.

☐ c. The tragedy was caused by nature and by human error.

5. In which paragraph did you find your information or details to answer question 3? _____

_____ Number of correct answers

Record your personal assessment of your work on the Critical Thinking Chart on page 58.

Personal Response

How do you think you would feel if you were Michael Dopheide, the man who rescued more than 30 people?

_____

_____

_____

Self-Assessment

The part I found most difficult about the article was _____.

_____

I found this difficult because _____

_____

_____

_____

Nightmare in the Twin Towers

It had been a great field trip. The 17 six-year-olds had just seen all of New York City. They had viewed it from the top of the World Trade Center. The center has two huge towers. Each rises 110 stories into the air. The children had been at the top of the south tower.

2   Now they were headed back down. For them, even an elevator ride was thrilling. The ride was supposed to take just 90 seconds. As it turned out, though, it took much longer. And

The World Trade Center in New York City was rocked by a terrorist bomb blast on February 26, 1993. Emergency workers rushed to the scene to rescue the approximately 100,000 people inside.

it was more than a thrill. It was a nightmare.

3   The date was February 26, 1993. The teacher led the children into the elevator. It was a big car, 10 feet by 20 feet. But there were lots of other people going down. By the time the doors closed, the car was very full. There were 72 people inside. "We were really squashed," said one woman, who was helping with the field trip. "But we only thought it was going to be a few minutes."

4   The kids began counting the floors as they zipped past. Halfway down, the lights over the door flickered and died. "Then all of a sudden—boom!" said one passenger. It was exactly 12:18 P.M. "[The elevator] stopped. All the kids screamed." The car was stuck between the 36th and the 35th floors.

5   There was no room to move about. The car was pitch black. The only light came from cigarette lighters. The adults tried to calm the small children. A few older children in the car, however, started to panic. One cried, "I am going to die. That's it. I am going to die."

6   To distract the kids, the adults led them in song. The children sang everything they knew. They sang alphabet songs. They sang holiday songs. They also sang the theme song from the TV show Barney. The kids did their best to belt out, "I love you, you love me, we're a happy family."

7   With so many people packed together, the car grew hotter and hotter. Then, somehow, the passengers pried the doors open a bit. That let in some fresh air. But it also revealed a terrible sight. Smoke was curling up the elevator shaft. Now, even some of the adults began to lose hope. "I thought we were all going to die," said one passenger.

8   At last, after four long hours, rescue workers reached the car. They passed a flashlight inside. Then they set up a special ladder to get people out. It was a slow and difficult job. One hour later, just 10 children had been retrieved. Luckily, at that point, the car came to life again. It slowly resumed its downward journey. When it reached the ground floor, everyone inside shouted for joy. Few people have ever been happier to get out of an elevator.

9   But shocking news awaited them. The car had not stopped because of a power outage. It had not stopped because of some faulty part. It was far worse than that. There had been a huge explosion at the base of the tower. Terrorists had tried to blow up the World Trade Center.

10   They had almost succeeded. Two men had driven a rented van into the underground garage. They had with them a 1,200-pound bomb. They planted the bomb in the garage, then took off. The bomb exploded at 12:18.

11   The World Trade Center is like a small city. Every day 130,000 people go there to work or visit. The bombers had hoped to bring down the whole complex. That was why they used such a huge bomb. The blast was enormous. It swayed all 110 stories of both towers. It left a crater 200 feet by 100 feet. The hole was five stories deep. Yet, mercifully, neither tower collapsed.

12   Six people died in the blast. Given the bomb's size, it was a miracle that more didn't die. One firefighter stared in wonder at the massive crater. It was a sight he wouldn't soon forget. "It looked like a giant barbecue pit with coals burning," he said.

13   The blast injured more than 1,000 people. It blew out windows. It knocked out the lights and power in both towers. All the backup systems were ruined too. The blast shook marble slabs loose. Steam pipes ruptured, spewing hot mist into the air. Fires broke out. And thick, black smoke was drawn up through the stairways until it reached the top floors. One worker was on the 105th floor at the time of the blast. "All the computers shut down. All the phones shut down," he said. "Then all of a sudden we saw smoke everywhere."

14   Some people broke windows to let in fresh air. That was not a good idea. It vented the smoke, making it spread faster. Also, the pieces of broken glass injured people on the streets below.

15   It was even worse in the basement of the twin towers. Joseph Cacciatore worked there. The blast was so strong that it knocked out his contact lenses. It also shattered his eye socket. His face was splattered with blood. In the darkness, Cacciatore wasn't sure how badly he had been hurt. But he knew he wasn't the only one injured. All around him he could hear people screaming.

16   Firefighter Kevin Shea went to check out the parking garage. But the bomb had weakened the floor. As he inched his way along, the concrete gave way. Shea fell four floors. Incredibly, he wasn't killed. He landed on a pile of heavy cardboard, breaking only his left knee and right foot. Still, he thought he would die. "Rocks and cinders were falling everywhere," he said later. "I thought, 'This is it.' I prayed to God to take me quick."

17   The bomb rocked more than the World Trade Center. It rocked the nation. Americans were horrified by the attack. They pressed police to find out who had done this evil deed.

18   The police soon had the answer. A group of Muslim militants was arrested. Their leader was Sheik Omar Abdel-Rahman. He was a preacher who had always hated the United States. He had urged his followers to wage "holy war." The World Trade Center was just for starters. He had plans to blow up other New York City landmarks, as well. One was the United Nations building. Others were the Lincoln and Holland tunnels and the George Washington Bridge.

19   In the fall of 1993, 10 Muslims were brought to trial. The court found all of them guilty. Abdel-Rahman got life in prison. The nine other plotters received 25 years to life in prison. But the damage was done. The World Trade Center had to be closed for a month. And the memory of the bombing lingered long beyond that.

If you have been timed while reading this article, enter your reading time below. Then turn to the Words-per-Minute Table on page 55 and look up your reading speed (words per minute). Enter your reading speed on the graph on page 56.

Reading Time: Lesson 5

_____ : _____
Minutes   Seconds

A | Finding the Main Idea

One statement below expresses the main idea of the article. One statement is too general, or too broad. The other statement explains only part of the article; it is too narrow. Label the statements using the following key:

M—Main Idea   **B—Too Broad**   **N—Too Narrow**

_____ 1. Terrorist attacks around the world have injured and killed private citizens and have destroyed important public gathering places.

_____ 2. The crater created by the terrorist bomb measured about 200 feet by 100 feet and was about five stories deep.

_____ 3. A 1993 terrorist bombing at the World Trade Center in New York City killed six people, injured more than 1,000 others, and caused heavy damage to the building.

_____ Score 15 points for a correct M answer.

_____ Score 5 points for each correct B or N answer.

_____ **Total Score:** Finding the Main Idea

B | Recalling Facts

How well do you remember the facts in the article? Put an X in the box next to the answer that correctly completes each statement about the article.

1. The World Trade Center has
   - ☐ a. 35 floors.
   - ☐ b. 110 floors.
   - ☐ c. 300 floors.

2. On a typical day, the center held about
   - ☐ a. 1,300 people.
   - ☐ b. 13,000 people.
   - ☐ c. 130,000 people.

3. The bomb was planted
   - ☐ a. in a huge garage.
   - ☐ b. on the roof.
   - ☐ c. in the elevator shaft.

4. Another planned target of the bombers was the
   - ☐ a. Golden Gate Bridge.
   - ☐ b. United Nations building.
   - ☐ c. Grand Canyon.

5. The militants' leader, Abdel-Rahman, was found guilty of the bombing and was sentenced to
   - ☐ a. life in prison.
   - ☐ b. 25 years in prison.
   - ☐ c. death.

Score 5 points for each correct answer.

_____ **Total Score:** Recalling Facts

C Making Inferences

When you combine your own experience with information from a text to draw a conclusion that is not directly stated in that text, you are making an inference. Below are five statements that may or may not be inferences based on information in the article. Label the statements using the following key:

C—Correct Inference   **F—Faulty Inference**

_____ 1. The people in the World Trade Center were totally surprised by the bombing.

_____ 2. About five hours after the bombing, some of the electricity in the building came back on.

_____ 3. All vehicles entering the parking garage at the World Trade Center were inspected carefully.

_____ 4. The emergency rooms in New York City hospitals were busy for hours after the explosion.

_____ 5. The explosion showed that the towers were poorly built.

Score 5 points for each correct answer.

_____ **Total Score**: Making Inferences

D Using Words Precisely

Each numbered sentence below contains an underlined word or phrase from the article. Following the sentence are three definitions. One definition is closest to the meaning of the underlined word. One definition is opposite or nearly opposite. Label those two definitions using the following key; do not label the remaining definition.

C—Closest   **O—Opposite or Nearly Opposite**

1. Halfway down, the lights over the door <u>flickered</u> and died.

_____ a. shone steadily

_____ b. sizzled

_____ c. blinked

2. But it also <u>revealed</u> a terrible sight.

_____ a. hid

_____ b. opened up to view

_____ c. imagined

3. One hour later, just 10 children had been <u>retrieved</u>.

_____ a. remembered

_____ b. left behind

_____ c. rescued; brought back

4. Steam pipes <u>ruptured</u>, spewing hot mist into the air.

_____ a. broke apart

_____ b. whistled

_____ c. came together

5. A group of Muslim <u>militants</u> was arrested.

_____ a. foreigners

_____ b. those who fight to support a cause

_____ c. peaceful people who refuse to fight

_____ Score 3 points for each correct C answer.

_____ Score 2 points for each correct O answer.

_____ **Total Score:** Using Words Precisely

Enter the four total scores in the spaces below, and add them together to find your Reading Comprehension Score. Then record your score on the graph on page 57.

Score	Question Type	Lesson 5
_____	Finding the Main Idea	
_____	Recalling Facts	
_____	Making Inferences	
_____	Using Words Precisely	
_____	**Reading Comprehension Score**	

Author's Approach

Put an X in the box next to the correct answer.

1. What is the authors' purpose in writing "Nightmare in the Twin Towers"?

   ☐ a. to encourage the reader to take the stairs instead of an elevator

   ☐ b. to inform the reader about a shocking explosion that caused panic

   ☐ c. to express an opinion about violence

2. Which of the following statements from the article best describes what the adults on the stalled elevator car found most frightening?

   ☐ a. The car was pitch black. The only light came from cigarette lighters.

   ☐ b. With so many people packed together, the car grew hotter and hotter.

   ☐ c. Smoke was curling up the elevator shaft.

3. In this article, "The bomb rocked more than the World Trade Center. It rocked the nation" means

   ☐ a. U.S. citizens were extremely frightened and angry about the explosion.

   ☐ b. the explosion was felt all over the United States.

   ☐ c. this explosion caused more explosions in other parts of the country.

_____ Number of correct answers

Record your personal assessment of your work on the Critical Thinking Chart on page 58.

Summarizing and Paraphrasing

Follow the directions provided for questions 1 and 2. Put an X in the box next to the correct answer for question 3.

1. Look for the important ideas and events in paragraphs 19 and 20. Summarize those paragraphs in one or two sentences.

   _____

   _____

   _____

   _____

2. Complete the following one-sentence summary of the article using the lettered phrases from the phrase bank below. Write the letters on the lines.

   ### Phrase Bank
   a. the experiences of a class of six-year-olds at the World Trade Center
   b. what had caused the explosion and how the blast affected various individuals
   c. the trial and sentencing of the terrorists

   The article "Nightmare in the Twin Towers" begins with

   _____, goes on to explain _____, and ends with

   _____.

3. Read the statement from the article below. Then read the paraphrase of that statement. Choose the reason that best tells why the paraphrase does not say the same thing as the statement.

   Statement: The leader of the terrorists planned to blow up other New York City landmarks, such as the United Nations building.

   Paraphrase: Other places in New York City, such as the United Nations building, were also blown up by the terrorists.

   ☐ a. Paraphrase says too much.

   ☐ b. Paraphrase doesn't say enough.

   ☐ c. Paraphrase doesn't agree with the statement.

   _____ Number of correct answers

   Record your personal assessment of your work on the Critical Thinking Chart on page 58.

Critical Thinking

Put an X in the box next to the correct answer for the following questions.

1. Which of the following statements from the article is an opinion rather than a fact?

   ☐ a. Few people have ever been happier to get out of an elevator.

   ☐ b. Some people broke windows to let in fresh air.

   ☐ c. There had been a huge explosion at the base of the tower.

2. From what the article told about what happened to the children on their elevator ride, you can predict that

   ☐ a. most of them will hope that an experience like that will happen to them again.

   ☐ b. many of them will be nervous about getting onto an elevator in the future.

   ☐ c. they will never go on a field trip again.

3. What were the effects of breaking windows to let fresh air into the building?

   ☐ a. People on the streets below were injured by broken glass.

   ☐ b. People were able to call for help.

   ☐ c. The fire spread more quickly.

4. What did you have to do to answer question 2?

   ☐ a. find an opinion (what someone thinks about something)

   ☐ b. find a description (how something looks)

   ☐ c. make a prediction (what will happen next)

_____ Number of correct answers

Record your personal assessment of your work on the Critical Thinking Chart on page 58.

Personal Response

If you could ask the authors of the article one question, what would it be?

_____

_____

_____

Self-Assessment

When reading the article, I was having trouble with _____

_____

_____

_____

Compare and Contrast

Think about the articles you have read in Unit One. Pick three articles that describe situations that could have been prevented if someone had acted differently. Write the titles of those articles in the first column of the chart below. Use information you learned from the articles to fill in the empty boxes in the chart.

Title	Where did the disaster take place?	Who or what caused the disaster?	How did victims react to the situation?

Here is one way in which the disaster described in the article _____ could have been prevented or at least made less harmful: _____

_____

_____

Words-per-Minute Table

Unit One

Directions: If you were timed while reading an article, refer to the Reading Time you recorded in the box at the end of the article. Use this Words-per-Minute Table to determine your reading speed for that article. Then plot your reading speed on the graph on page 56.

Lesson / No. of Words	Sample 693	1 1,050	2 1,097	3 1,022	4 1,084	5 1,127	Seconds
1:30	462	700	731	681	723	751	**90**
1:40	416	630	658	613	650	676	**100**
1:50	378	573	598	557	591	615	**110**
2:00	347	525	549	511	542	564	**120**
2:10	320	485	506	472	500	520	**130**
2:20	297	450	470	438	465	483	**140**
2:30	277	420	439	409	434	451	**150**
2:40	260	394	411	383	407	423	**160**
2:50	245	371	387	361	383	398	**170**
3:00	231	350	366	341	361	376	**180**
3:10	219	332	346	323	342	356	**190**
3:20	208	315	329	307	325	338	**200**
3:30	198	300	313	292	310	322	**210**
3:40	189	286	299	279	296	307	**220**
3:50	181	274	286	267	283	294	**230**
4:00	173	263	274	256	271	282	**240**
4:10	166	252	263	245	260	270	**250**
4:20	160	242	253	236	250	260	**260**
4:30	154	233	244	227	241	250	**270**
4:40	149	225	235	219	232	242	**280**
4:50	143	217	227	211	224	233	**290**
5:00	139	210	219	204	217	225	**300**
5:10	134	203	212	198	210	218	**310**
5:20	130	197	206	192	203	211	**320**
5:30	126	191	199	186	197	205	**330**
5:40	122	185	194	180	191	199	**340**
5:50	119	180	188	175	186	193	**350**
6:00	116	175	183	170	181	188	**360**
6:10	112	170	178	166	176	183	**370**
6:20	109	166	173	161	171	178	**380**
6:30	107	162	169	157	167	173	**390**
6:40	104	158	165	153	163	169	**400**
6:50	101	154	161	150	159	165	**410**
7:00	99	150	157	146	155	161	**420**
7:10	97	147	153	143	151	157	**430**
7:20	95	143	150	139	148	154	**440**
7:30	92	140	146	136	145	150	**450**
7:40	90	137	143	133	141	147	**460**
7:50	88	134	140	130	138	144	**470**
8:00	87	131	137	128	136	141	**480**

Minutes and Seconds (left axis label) / *Seconds* (right axis label)

Plotting Your Progress: Reading Speed

Unit One

Directions: If you were timed while reading an article, write your words-per-minute rate for that article in the box under the number of the lesson. Then plot your reading speed on the graph by putting a small X on the line directly above the number of the lesson, across from the number of words per minute you read. As you mark your speed for each lesson, graph your progress by drawing a line to connect the X's.

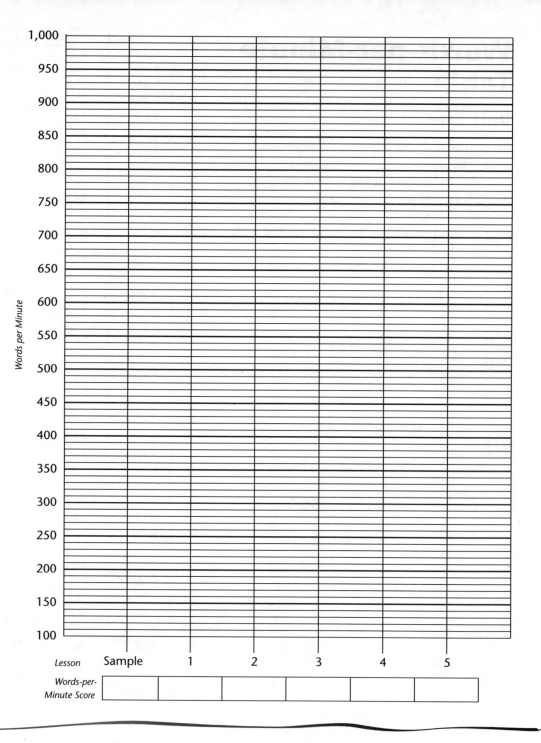

Plotting Your Progress: Reading Comprehension

Unit One

Directions: Write your Reading Comprehension score for each lesson in the box under the number of the lesson. Then plot your score on the graph by putting a small X on the line directly above the number of the lesson and across from the score you earned. As you mark your score for each lesson, graph your progress by drawing a line to connect the X's.

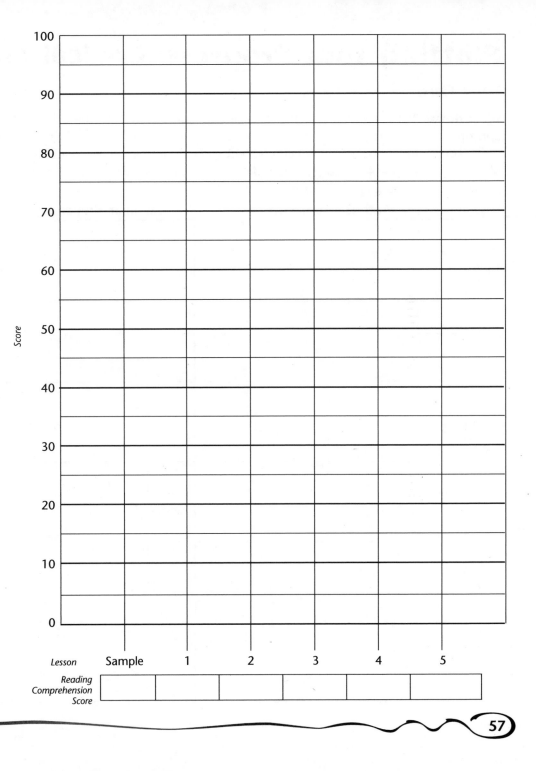

Lesson	Sample	1	2	3	4	5
Reading Comprehension Score						

Plotting Your Progress: Critical Thinking

Unit One

Directions: Work with your teacher to evaluate your responses to the Critical Thinking questions for each lesson. Then fill in the appropriate spaces in the chart below. For each lesson and each type of Critical Thinking question, do the following: Mark a minus sign (–) in the box to indicate areas in which you feel you could improve. Mark a plus sign (+) to indicate areas in which you feel you did well. Mark a minus-slash-plus sign (–/+) to indicate areas in which you had mixed success. Then write any comments you have about your performance, including ideas for improvement.

Lesson	Author's Approach	Summarizing and Paraphrasing	Critical Thinking
Sample			
1			
2			
3			
4			
5			

UNIT TWO

Stay Out of the Water!

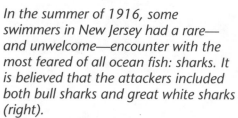

In the summer of 1916, some swimmers in New Jersey had a rare—and unwelcome—encounter with the most feared of all ocean fish: sharks. It is believed that the attackers included both bull sharks and great white sharks (right).

We will never know what Charles Vansant was thinking as he splashed in the water on that hot summer day. But chances are, he wasn't thinking about sharks. Most people in 1916 knew little about sharks. Many people believed that sharks were as harmless as other fish in the sea. Besides, people thought, sharks stayed in warm water. One would never travel as far north as, say, New Jersey.

2 Vansant took his swim at 5:00 P.M. on July 2, 1916. He was at Beach Haven, New Jersey. A man named Sheridan Taylor saw him standing alone in five feet of water. All at once, Vansant screamed. He began to beat the water wildly. Taylor saw the water around Vansant turn red. Quickly, Taylor swam out to help. As he drew near, he saw a shark biting into Vansant's leg. Taylor and some other men managed to drag Vansant to the beach. But it was too late. Charles Vansant died within a few hours.

3 Taylor and the other rescuers saw the shark clearly. They described it as 10 feet long and bluish-gray. But experts dismissed the men's claim. These experts said it could not possibly have been a shark. Surely, they said, the men were mistaken. Surely it had been some other kind of fish.

4 Four days later, a man named Charles Bruder went swimming at a beach called Spring Lake. It was 35 miles north of Beach Haven. Without warning, Bruder, too, was struck by a shark. It attacked his right leg, biting the limb off just below the knee. The shark then ripped into Bruder's left leg. Rescuers got him to shore. But, again, it was too late. Bruder bled to death on the beach.

5 In the days following Bruder's death, the people of New Jersey grew frantic. Two people were dead, and the killer or killers were still at large. Most residents refused to return to the water. Officials tried to calm everyone's nerves. They put up wire nets along the beaches to keep sharks out. People began to patrol the shore in boats. They carried rifles, spears, and dynamite. Even so, most people didn't feel safe. Most swimmers stayed out of the ocean.

6 Meanwhile, the experts continued to get it wrong. Some still doubted that the killer was a shark. They said it might have been a very large turtle or a huge mackerel. Frank Claret, a boat captain, said he had never seen a man-eating shark north of the Bahamas. Olympic swimmer Annette Kellerman also spoke out on the subject. She proclaimed, "The shark, no matter what species he belongs to, is at heart an arrant coward. . . ."

7 Still, most people scanned the shore nervously. Some headed inland. They cooled off in rivers and bays. On July 12, Thomas Cottrell was fishing in Matawan Creek. He noticed a "dark, gray shape" moving through the water at a fast rate. Cottrell rushed into town to warn people that a shark was in the creek. But the townspeople merely laughed at him. The creek was 10 miles from the open ocean. How could any shark get that far inland? Besides, it was a hot day. Many people were determined to cool down in Matawan Creek.

8 Twelve-year-old Lester Stilwell was one of those people. Stilwell and some other boys took off for a swim in the creek. They decided to swim off an old pier. Stilwell was a strong swimmer. So he swam out further than his friends. Suddenly, out of nowhere, a shark grabbed the boy and pulled him down. When Stilwell surfaced again, he was flailing his arms and screaming. His body was swirling around and around in the water.

9 Stanley Fisher, aged 24, was standing nearby. He saw Stilwell struggling. Quickly Fisher ran to the edge of the creek. As he dashed past a woman, she shouted, "Remember what Cottrell said! It may have been a shark!"

10 "A shark here?" answered Fisher in disbelief. "I don't care, anyway. I'm going after that boy!"

11 Fisher jumped into his bathing suit and swam out to Stilwell. By then, the boy had been dragged underwater again. Fisher dove down, searching for him. At last he came up to the surface, shouting, "I've got him!" By that time, Fisher was close to the opposite shore, so that's where he headed with the lifeless body of Lester Stilwell. He almost made it. His feet touched the bottom of the creek. Then, in one terrible flash, the shark attacked him. People watching on the opposite shore saw Fisher throw up his arms and

yell. With its teeth locked into his flesh, the shark dragged Fisher underwater.

12 Other men, who were rushing to help in motorboats, managed to pull Fisher out of the water. He was still alive, but he was in shock. His right leg had been torn to shreds. There was no flesh left between his waist and knee. Fisher mumbled a few words, saying he had thought he was safe when his feet touched bottom. He died before reaching the hospital.

13 People were in a frenzy. Word of the shark attacks traveled like lightning up and down the banks of the creek. Everyone scrambled to get out of the water. John Dunn, aged 12, and some friends were diving off a pier when they heard the news. They hurried to climb to safety. Dunn was the last one out. With just his left leg still in the water, he felt a shark grab him. The creature tore away most of the boy's leg. Dunn was taken to the hospital. He lived, but his leg had to be amputated.

14 The attacks in Matawan Creek set off a massive shark hunt. Hundreds of hunters took to the water in boats. They armed themselves with nets, dynamite, guns, and hooks. Over the next two days, they scoured the New Jersey coastline. They managed to kill several sharks. One was an eight-and-one-half-foot great white shark. In its stomach lay human bones and flesh.

One bone was identified as the shinbone of Charles Bruder.

15 So there was no doubt about it: a shark really was to blame for the recent deaths. But was there only one killer, or were there others? At the time, most people thought all the attacks were the work of one crazed shark. We now know that that is not likely. A great white shark would never swim into an inland creek. The deadly bull shark, however, loves shallow water. So there were probably several dangerous sharks off the coast of New Jersey that summer. Luckily, though, the attacks stopped after the great white was killed. In time, life went back to normal for people in the area. But residents never again thought of sharks as "harmless."

If you have been timed while reading this article, enter your reading time below. Then turn to the Words-per-Minute Table on page 101 and look up your reading speed (words per minute). Enter your reading speed on the graph on page 102.

Reading Time: Lesson 6

_____ : _____
Minutes   Seconds

A | Finding the Main Idea

One statement below expresses the main idea of the article. One statement is too general, or too broad. The other statement explains only part of the article; it is too narrow. Label the statements using the following key:

M—Main Idea **B—Too Broad** **N—Too Narrow**

_____ 1. Certain types of sharks have been reported to kill or attack not only human beings swimming in oceans, but also those swimming in rivers that feed into the oceans.

_____ 2. It was probably a bull shark that entered the shallow water of Matawan Creek in 1916 and attacked swimmers there.

_____ 3. In July of 1916, two or more sharks terrorized the coast of New Jersey, attacking swimmers on the ocean beach and in a creek flowing into the ocean.

_____ Score 15 points for a correct M answer.

_____ Score 5 points for each correct B or N answer.

_____ **Total Score:** Finding the Main Idea

B | Recalling Facts

How well do you remember the facts in the article? Put an X in the box next to the answer that correctly completes each statement about the article.

1. The first New Jersey swimmer killed by sharks in the summer of 1916 was attacked
   ☐ a. near the shore at Beach Haven.
   ☐ b. near a beach called Spring Lake.
   ☐ c. in the waters of Matawan Creek.

2. After two swimmers were killed, officials
   ☐ a. put up wire nets along the beaches.
   ☐ b. hired professional shark hunters.
   ☐ c. told people to swim in large groups to be safe.

3. Some experts suggested that the killer was
   ☐ a. a whale.
   ☐ b. a large turtle.
   ☐ c. an alligator.

4. The man who tried to rescue a boy from a shark was himself attacked by the shark as he
   ☐ a. came close to the boy's body.
   ☐ b. pulled the boy's body from the fish.
   ☐ c. felt his feet touch the bottom of the creek.

5. Today, experts studying the 1916 attacks believe
   ☐ a. they were the work of one crazed killer.
   ☐ b. two or more sharks were responsible.
   ☐ c. all the reports were inaccurate.

Score 5 points for each correct answer.

_____ **Total Score:** Recalling Facts

C | Making Inferences

When you combine your own experience with information from a text to draw a conclusion that is not directly stated in that text, you are making an inference. Below are five statements that may or may not be inferences based on information in the article. Label the statements using the following key:

C—Correct Inference　　　**F—Faulty Inference**

_____ 1. If the victims of the 1916 shark attacks had been strong swimmers, they would not have been attacked.

_____ 2. Scientists and the public have learned a great deal more about sharks since 1916.

_____ 3. In 1916, at least some U.S. citizens knew that there were such things as man-eating sharks.

_____ 4. A shark can quickly and easily digest almost anything, including bones.

_____ 5. Shark attacks along the New Jersey coast, such as those in 1916, cannot happen today.

Score 5 points for each correct answer.

_____ **Total Score:** Making Inferences

D | Using Words Precisely

Each numbered sentence below contains an underlined word or phrase from the article. Following the sentence are three definitions. One definition is closest to the meaning of the underlined word. One definition is opposite or nearly opposite. Label those two definitions using the following key; do not label the remaining definition.

C—Closest　　　**O—Opposite or Nearly Opposite**

1. Most <u>residents</u> refused to return to the water.

_____ a. people who live in the area

_____ b. travelers; those passing through

_____ c. people who enjoy water sports

2. People began to <u>patrol</u> the shore in boats.

_____ a. ignore; disregard

_____ b. guard; watch

_____ c. invade

3. She proclaimed, "The shark, no matter what species he belongs to, is at heart an <u>arrant</u> coward."

_____ a. ignorant

_____ b. extreme

_____ c. hidden; secret

4. When Stilwell surfaced again, he was <u>flailing</u> his arms and screaming.

_____ a. holding still

_____ b. crossing

_____ c. waving

5. Over the next two days, they <u>scoured</u> the New Jersey coastline.

_____ a. frightened

_____ b. skimmed

_____ c. searched thoroughly

_____ Score 3 points for each correct C answer.

_____ Score 2 points for each correct O answer.

_____ **Total Score:** Using Words Precisely

Enter the four total scores in the spaces below, and add them together to find your Reading Comprehension Score. Then record your score on the graph on page 103.

Score	Question Type	Lesson 6
_____	Finding the Main Idea	
_____	Recalling Facts	
_____	Making Inferences	
_____	Using Words Precisely	
_____	**Reading Comprehension Score**	

Author's Approach

Put an X in the box next to the correct answer.

1. What do the authors mean by the statement "Many people believed that sharks were as harmless as other fish in the sea"?

☐ a. Not much research had been done about sharks at that time.

☐ b. People in the early 20th century were not as intelligent as people today.

☐ c. Sharks swimming off the coast of New Jersey in the early 20th century were less violent than sharks of today.

2. From the statements below, choose those that you believe the authors would agree with.

☐ a. Sharks can be dangerous to humans.

☐ b. Sharks never attack unless they are provoked, or bothered.

☐ c. Scientists don't know all the answers about nature.

3. The authors probably wrote this article to

☐ a. inform readers about a series of shark attacks that took place in New Jersey in 1916.

☐ b. teach readers about the habits of sharks.

☐ c. discourage people from swimming anywhere but in a swimming pool.

_____ Number of correct answers

Record your personal assessment of your work on the Critical Thinking Chart on page 104.

Summarizing and Paraphrasing

Put an X in the box next to the correct answer for questions 1 and 3. Follow the directions provided for question 2.

1. Below are summaries of the article. Choose the summary that says all the most important things about the article but in the fewest words.

☐ a. In 1916 Stanley Fisher sacrificed his own life to help a 12-year-old boy who was being attacked by a shark. Unfortunately, both the boy and Fisher died as a result of this shark attack in an inland creek.

☐ b. Even though people in New Jersey in the summer of 1916 reported being attacked by sharks, experts refused to believe their stories. Most people at that time believed that the shark was a harmless fish.

☐ c. A series of shark attacks caused panic in New Jersey in 1916. Sharks attacked swimmers in the ocean and in Matawan Creek until hunters killed several sharks. These attacks convinced people that sharks are dangerous.

2. Reread paragraph 8 in the article. Below, write a summary of the paragraph in no more than 25 words.

_____

_____

_____

_____

Reread your summary and decide whether it covers the important ideas in the paragraph. Next, decide how to shorten the summary to 15 words or less without leaving out any essential information. Write this summary below.

_____

_____

_____

3. Choose the best one-sentence paraphrase for the following sentence from the article "Word of the shark attacks traveled like lightning up and down the banks of the creek."

☐ a. Lightning strikes and shark attacks happened up and down the banks of the creek.

☐ b. People who were swimming in the creek very soon knew about the shark attack.

☐ c. People said that the shark struck like lightning up and down the creek banks.

_____ Number of correct answers

Record your personal assessment of your work on the Critical Thinking Chart on page 104.

Critical Thinking

Put an X in the box next to the correct answer for questions 1, 2, and 4. Follow the directions provided for question 3.

1. Which of the following statements from the article is an opinion rather than a fact?

   ☐ a. Vansant took his swim at 5:00 P.M. on July 2, 1916.

   ☐ b. The creek was 10 miles from the open ocean.

   ☐ c. The shark, no matter what species he belongs to, is at heart an arrant coward. . . .

2. From what Annette Kellerman said, you can predict that after human bones were found in a shark's stomach, she

   ☐ a. refused to change her mind about the shark's cowardice.

   ☐ b. felt embarrassed to have said that sharks are cowards.

   ☐ c. took full responsibility for the deaths of the swimmers who listened to her words and went swimming anyway.

3. Choose from the letters below to correctly complete the following statement. Write the letters on the lines.

   On the positive side, _____, but on the negative side, _____.

   a. several people died during the rash of shark attacks

   b. the shark attacks eventually stopped

   c. no one expected that sharks would swim into Matawan Creek

4. What did you have to do to answer question 3?

   ☐ a. find a contrast (how things are different)

   ☐ b. find a description (how something looks)

   ☐ c. find an effect (something that happened)

_____ Number of correct answers

Record your personal assessment of your work on the Critical Thinking Chart on page 104.

Personal Response

Would you recommend this article to other students? Explain.

_____

_____

_____

Self-Assessment

One good question about this article that was not asked would be,

_____

_____

And the answer is _____

_____

_____

A Sniper in the Tower

The note began, "To whom it may concern." On July 31, 1966, Charles Whitman wrote this note as his last message to the world. The 25-year-old University of Texas student knew he did not have long to live. "I am prepared to die," he wrote. He went on to say more. "I intend to kill my wife. I don't want her to face the embarrassment that my actions will surely cause her."

On one terrible July afternoon in 1966, the normally peaceful Austin campus of the University of Texas rang out with gunfire. Charles Whitman stood on the observation tower with a loaded rifle and shot at human targets across the entire campus.

2   What actions? Whitman had hinted at the answer four months earlier. He had gone to see psychiatrist Maurice Heatly. Whitman told Dr. Heatly he feared his own "violent impulses." He confessed to beating his wife, Kathy, more than once. Then he said something even scarier. He described his urge to go up to the top of a school tower "with a deer rifle and start shooting people."

3   Heatly later said that Whitman had been "oozing with hostility." But Heatly wasn't alarmed. Lots of students, he said, say crazy things. Most of them don't mean it. Heatly told Whitman to come back for another visit. (Whitman never did.) Beyond that, Heatly did nothing.

4   Who was Charles Whitman? And why was he so angry? Most people who knew him had no clue. Whitman kept his anger well hidden. To the outside world, he was an "All-American boy." He was an Eagle Scout at the age of 12. He was an altar boy in church. Whitman also had a paper route and played sports. "He was a nice little boy," recalled one neighbor.

5   As a young adult, Whitman became a Boy Scout leader. The children loved him. "Why, I remember last summer when he had to go away," said one parent. "My son cried because Charlie wouldn't be around."

6   But there was another Charles Whitman. In his final note, he wrote how he hated his father "with a mortal passion." Over the years, he had often seen his father beat his mother. Just recently, Whitman's mother had moved out. When she did, Charles Whitman called the police to keep watch over her. He feared that his father might show up and get violent.

7   But it was the son, not the father, who turned out to be a killer. On the night of July 31, Whitman went to his mother's apartment. He killed her. Then he added some lines to his note. "I have just killed my mother," he wrote. "If there's a heaven, she is going there. If there's not a heaven, she is out of her pain and misery. I love my mother with all my heart."

8   Whitman then returned to his home. He murdered his wife as she lay sleeping. The next day, Whitman took out his rage on the rest of the world. He climbed to the top of the University of Texas tower. It was the tallest building in Austin. Dressed as a repairman, Whitman took the elevator to the 27th floor. He had a footlocker with him. Inside, he had stuffed food, water, knives, guns, and hundreds of bullets.

9   Whitman dragged the footlocker up the last few stairs to the top floor. He planned to go out onto the observation deck. A woman was sitting at a desk next to the door. Her name was Edna Townsley. She never had a chance. Whitman hit her over the head with a rifle butt. Then he shot her and dragged her body behind a sofa. She died a few hours later.

10   As Whitman unpacked his arsenal, six people came walking up the stairs. It was a family who just wanted to see the view. Whitman heard them coming. Quickly, he grabbed a gun and started shooting. Two of the people fell back down the stairs, dead. Two others were badly wounded. The remaining two tried to help the wounded. Whitman then went to the top of the stairs and slammed the door shut.

11   It was 11:48 A.M. when Whitman got out onto the observation deck. The walkway was six feet wide and went all the way around the tower. Through the scope on his rifle, Whitman could see

the whole campus. With a cool and deadly aim, he opened fire. He moved around the tower, shooting in all directions. Clearly, he wanted to kill people—lots of people.

12   At first, no one down below knew what the odd puffs of smoke from the tower meant. Then people started falling. Still, it took a few moments for others to understand that there was a sniper on the tower.

13   Norma Barger heard loud noises and looked out her window. She saw six bodies lying on the ground. She thought it was a student prank. "I expected the six to get up and walk away laughing." Then she saw the blood. Only then did Barger realize it was no joke.

14   Pat Sonntag was strolling across the lawn with Claudia Rutt. The two were holding hands. Suddenly, Claudia crumpled to the ground. "Help me," she cried out. As Pat bent over to see what was wrong with her, the sniper fired another bullet. Pat collapsed over Claudia's body. Both were mortally wounded.

15   Robert Boyer was shot and killed on his way to lunch. Thomas Karr had spent all night studying for a big test. He was headed home for a short nap when Whitman gunned him down.

Thomas Aston was walking on the roof of a nearby building. Whitman killed him too. Roy Dell Schmidt, who was three blocks away, heard the shooting, then clutched his chest and fell dead. "He told me we were out of range," said a man who had been standing next to him.

16   The police soon arrived. One of the first was Officer Billy Speed. He took cover behind some stone columns. But the sniper saw a slight opening between the columns. He killed Speed with one bullet. Soon many other officers arrived. They poured heavy fire at the tower. That forced Whitman to keep his head down. Still, he could fire through the drain openings around the base of the tower. So he was able to keep up his deadly fire. Before long the campus was littered with the dead and wounded.

17   During Whitman's stay in the tower, he killed 13 people. He wounded 31 others. One victim was Claire Wilson, who was eight months pregnant. Claire survived, but her baby did not.

18   Whitman's reign of terror lasted more than an hour and a half. No one could kill him from the ground. At last, four men decided to go into the building, hoping to get him from in there. The men were led by Romero Martinez, an

off-duty police officer. They took the elevator to the 27th floor. Then they walked up the stairs past the spot where the first four people had been shot. The men opened the door and crept out onto the observation deck. Martinez inched his way in one direction. A man named Allen Crum went the other way. Crum fired some shots to distract Whitman. It worked. Martinez caught Whitman by surprise and shot him dead.

19   At last the nightmare was over. The terror subsided. But the grief lasted much longer. For the families of the victims, nothing would ever be the same again.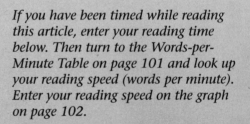

A Finding the Main Idea

One statement below expresses the main idea of the article. One statement is too general, or too broad. The other statement explains only part of the article; it is too narrow. Label the statements using the following key:

M—Main Idea   **B—Too Broad**   **N—Too Narrow**

_____ 1. In a little over one and a half hours, Charles Whitman killed 13 people and wounded 31 others in a several-block area.

_____ 2. On August 1, 1966, after killing his wife and his mother, a student at the University of Texas at Austin shot people in and around the campus tower, killing 13.

_____ 3. On August 1, 1966, the Austin campus of the University of Texas was the scene of a tragic occurrence in which many people died.

_____ Score 15 points for a correct M answer.

_____ Score 5 points for each correct B or N answer.

_____ **Total Score:** Finding the Main Idea

B Recalling Facts

How well do you remember the facts in the article? Put an X in the box next to the answer that correctly completes each statement about the article.

1. The first person Charles Whitman killed was
   ☐ a. his mother.
   ☐ b. his wife.
   ☐ c. an office worker at the tower.

2. Whitman had talked to a psychiatrist
   ☐ a. four months earlier.
   ☐ b. a month earlier.
   ☐ c. a day before the shootings.

3. One of Whitman's secret fears was
   ☐ a. a fear of high places.
   ☐ b. worry about atomic war.
   ☐ c. that his father might hurt his mother.

4. Whitman said that he killed his wife and his mother because he
   ☐ a. loved them.
   ☐ b. hated them.
   ☐ c. wanted their insurance money.

5. Whitman was finally killed by
   ☐ a. hanging, after a long trial.
   ☐ b. police flying a helicopter over the tower.
   ☐ c. a police officer who climbed the tower and entered the observation deck where he was.

Score 5 points for each correct answer.

_____ **Total Score:** Recalling Facts

C | Making Inferences

When you combine your own experience with information from a text to draw a conclusion that is not directly stated in that text, you are making an inference. Below are five statements that may or may not be inferences based on information in the article. Label the statements using the following key:

C—Correct Inference   **F—Faulty Inference**

_____ 1. The top floor of the University of Texas tower was popular with sightseers.

_____ 2. Charles Whitman believed that people preferred to be dead rather than embarrassed.

_____ 3. Sometime before his shooting spree, Whitman recognized that he needed help.

_____ 4. Whitman knew all of his victims personally and was taking revenge on each of them for a past insult or injury.

_____ 5. In the United States, it is easy for a person with mental and emotional problems to get possession of guns and ammunition.

Score 5 points for each correct answer.

_____ **Total Score:** Making Inferences

D | Using Words Precisely

Each numbered sentence below contains an underlined word or phrase from the article. Following the sentence are three definitions. One definition is closest to the meaning of the underlined word. One definition is opposite or nearly opposite. Label those two definitions using the following key; do not label the remaining definition.

C—Closest   **O—Opposite or Nearly Opposite**

1. Whitman told Dr. Heatly he feared his "violent <u>impulses</u>."

_____ a. thought-out positions

_____ b. sudden, strong urges

_____ c. associates

2. Heatly later said that Whitman had been "oozing with hostility." But Heatly wasn't <u>alarmed</u>.

_____ a. calm

_____ b. helpful

_____ c. disturbed

3. In his final note, he wrote how he hated his father "with a mortal <u>passion</u>."

_____ a. emotion

_____ b. injury

_____ c. indifference

4. Pat collapsed over Claudia's body. Both were <u>mortally</u> wounded.

_____ a. obviously

_____ b. fatally

_____ c. slightly

5. Whitman's <u>reign of terror</u> lasted more than an hour and a half.

_____ a. time of violence

_____ b. period of calm

_____ c. time off

_____ Score 3 points for each correct C answer.

_____ Score 2 points for each correct O answer.

_____ **Total Score:** Using Words Precisely

Enter the four total scores in the spaces below, and add them together to find your Reading Comprehension Score. Then record your score on the graph on page 103.

Score	Question Type	Lesson 7
_____	Finding the Main Idea	
_____	Recalling Facts	
_____	Making Inferences	
_____	Using Words Precisely	
_____	**Reading Comprehension Score**	

Author's Approach

Put an X in the box next to the correct answer.

1. The main purpose of the first paragraph is to

☐ a. create a mood of suspense.

☐ b. express an opinion about Charles Whitman.

☐ c. compare Charles Whitman and his wife.

2. Judging by statements from the article "A Sniper in the Tower," you can conclude that the authors want the reader to think that

☐ a. Charles Whitman had always been violent and angry.

☐ b. Charles Whitman acted on the spur of the moment, without planning.

☐ c. Charles Whitman planned the shootings ahead of time.

3. What do the authors imply by saying "Dressed as a repairman, Whitman took the elevator to the 27th floor"?

☐ a. Whitman was hiding weapons in his repairman uniform.

☐ b. Whitman had always wanted to be a repairman and was acting out his dream.

☐ c. Whitman wanted to go unnoticed and to get into places most people aren't allowed to enter.

4. The authors probably wrote this article to

☐ a. encourage people to stay away from high towers.

☐ b. inform readers about a terrible, frightening event.

☐ c. show how easy it is to get into a restricted area.

_____ Number of correct answers

Record your personal assessment of your work on the Critical Thinking Chart on page 104.

Summarizing and Paraphrasing

Follow the directions provided for questions 1 and 2. Put an X in the box next to the correct answer for question 3.

1. Look for the important ideas and events in paragraphs 11 and 12. Summarize those paragraphs in one or two sentences.

_____

_____

_____

_____

2. Complete the following one-sentence summary of the article using the lettered phrases from the phrase bank below. Write the letters on the lines.

> **Phrase Bank**
> a. Charles Whitman's death
> b. the damage Charles Whitman caused on July 31
> c. a description of Charles Whitman's mental state before his shooting spree

The article "A Sniper in the Tower" begins with _____, goes

on to explain _____, and ends with _____.

3. Choose the sentence that correctly restates the following sentence from the article "To the outside world, [Whitman] was an 'All-American boy.'"

☐ a. To people from other countries, Whitman represented America.

☐ b. On the outside, Whitman looked like an American.

☐ c. On the surface, Whitman seemed like an average, well-behaved citizen.

> _____ Number of correct answers
>
> Record your personal assessment of your work on the Critical Thinking Chart on page 104.

Critical Thinking

Follow the directions provided for questions 1 and 4. Put an X in the box next to the correct answer for the other questions.

1. For each statement below, write *O* if it expresses an opinion or write *F* if it expresses a fact.

_____ a. It is sad that no one was able to stop Charles Whitman from killing so many people.

_____ b. Whitman stepped onto the observation deck at 11:48 A.M.

_____ c. Charles Whitman had once been a Boy Scout leader.

2. Judging by the events in the article, you can conclude that the following happened next:

☐ a. The university renamed the tower Whitman Tower.

☐ b. University security made it harder for people to take weapons onto the observation deck.

☐ c. Police apologized for shooting Whitman.

3. What was the cause of Whitman's decision to shoot his wife?

☐ a. He didn't want her to be embarrassed by his actions.

☐ b. He hated his wife.

☐ c. He knew he was going to die and he didn't want her living without him.

4. In which paragraph did you find your information or details to answer question 3? _____

_____ Number of correct answers

Record your personal assessment of your work on the Critical Thinking Chart on page 104.

Personal Response

How do you think Dr. Heatly felt when he learned that Whitman had gone on a shooting spree from the tower?

_____

_____

_____

_____

Self-Assessment

I can't really understand how _____

_____

_____

_____

The Night the Dam Let Go

The St. Francis Dam, which supplied water to Los Angeles, unexpectedly let go on the night of March 12, 1928. When the dam broke, 12 billion gallons of water spilled down the canyon below, killing at least 450 sleeping people.

Tony Harnischfeger did not like what he was seeing. The St. Francis Dam was discharging "dirty" water. As dam keeper, Harnischfeger knew the water should be clear. So he asked William Mulholland, the builder of the dam, to check it out. Mulholland inspected the dam. He pronounced it sound. He said there was no need to worry.

2   Later that same day, March 12, 1928, Bill Riley stopped by the dam. He, his wife Abigail, and their two daughters wanted to see the great St. Francis Dam. People called it an engineering marvel. Its walls were 200 feet high. They held back 12 billion gallons of water. The dam was a key source of water for the city of Los Angeles, 50 miles to the south.

3   Like Harnischfeger, Riley saw something he did not like. Water was seeping into the rocky soil at the foot of the dam. "This dam could go!" he warned his wife.

4   She just laughed at him. "Don't be silly," she said. "Those people wouldn't have built a dam that weak." Still, Riley didn't want to take any chances. He told his family to get back into the truck. Then he floored the gas pedal. "Bill broke every speed limit to get away," his wife said later.

5   Maybe Bill Riley just made a lucky guess. But he was right on the money. At 11:57 that evening, the dam gave way. First one side collapsed. Then the other side went. Finally the middle fell too. Twelve billion gallons of raging water poured over the crumbling walls of the dam. It was enough to form a wave 75 feet high.

6   The deadly wave roared down the San Francisquito Canyon. It wiped out more than 1,200 ranch houses that dotted the canyon. One writer wrote that homes were "crushed like egg shells." The water ripped up trees and washed away bridges. It also knocked out power lines and flooded all the towns in the valley.

7   Most inhabitants of the canyon were asleep when the dam broke. They had little chance to survive. The water engulfed many people in their beds. Some, however, heard the roar of the water as it approached. It sounded like a runaway freight train. People who heard it threw on their shoes and dashed for higher ground. Some made it; others did not.

8   John Haskell was one who heard the wild water coming. He rushed to warn his family, screaming, "The dam's gone out! We've got to find Clara and Oscar!" But it was too late. His aunt Clara Willmont was lost in the flood. Somehow his uncle Oscar survived. But the poor man was overcome with grief. The loss of his wife and other family members was more than he could take. A short time later, Oscar, too, died.

9   Some people survived by grabbing a piece of debris and riding with the flow of water. Eighty-year-old C. H. Hunick lived in a ranch house a mile and a half from the dam. "When the water hit it, the house crumbled as though it were built of cards," he later recalled. Hunick couldn't see anything in the darkness. But he managed to reach out and grab onto something.

10 It turned out to be a chunk of his own roof. "Down, down with the current we went," he said. "I kept saying to myself every second was my last. I knew that I could not last long. . . . My strength was going fast, but I hung on." Then, out of the darkness, an arm reached out and seized him.

11 "Is that you, Dad?" a voice shouted. It was Hunick's own son. The son pulled Hunick over onto the plank he was floating on. Later, the two men were rescued and taken to a hospital. There, C. H. Hunick began asking about his other two sons. Sadly, the doctors had to tell him that both had perished earlier that night in the flood.

12 Ann Holzcloth's home was also destroyed by the raging water. She was in bed with her baby when the wave struck. "I clutched him tight as we were swept out on the water in the dark," she said. She managed to grab a piece of floating lumber with one hand. "With my other arm, I held the baby out of the water the best I could." They soon hit a powerful whirlpool, however, and the force of the water ripped the baby from her grasp. The violent wave tossed Holzcloth up onto dry land. But it carried her son away. "Why did I have to live?" she wept.

13 Many other people died that awful night. Rescue workers found heartbreaking evidence of the victims'

final frantic moments. Most people died in their nightclothes. One little girl was wearing just one untied shoe. Others had had their clothing ripped off by the rushing water.

14 The death toll was set at 450. But the true count was probably much higher. Professor Doyce B. Nunis thinks it was more like 600. Nunis points out that many bodies "were washed into the ocean." Also, there were a number of migrant workers in the region. As Nunis notes, many of them "were never accounted for."

15 What caused the dam to break? The blame has always been pinned on William Mulholland. He was supposed to have built an "impregnable" master-piece. Instead, his dam crumbled after just two years. Some people claimed it had not been properly anchored in bedrock. They said that underground water had seeped into the dam and weakened it.

16 Before the dam's collapse, Mulholland was a local hero. He was the one who had used aqueducts and dams to bring water to parched Los Angeles. After the dam's collapse, however, people hated him. One woman hammered a sign into the front yard of her mud-filled home. The sign read: KILL MULHOLLAND.

17 Mulholland bravely took responsibility for the disaster. "Don't blame anyone else," he said. "You just fasten it on me.

If there is an error of human judgment, I was the human."

18 But was he really to blame? A 1995 book written by engineer J. David Rogers says no. According to Rogers, the dam was built on top of rubble from an ancient landslide. Mulholland had no way of knowing that. The rubble was too far underground to be detected. But the weight of the dam caused the rubble to shift. That, in turn, caused the dam to give way.

19 If Rogers is right, the bursting of the St. Francis Dam was not Mulholland's fault. But that is small comfort for families of the victims. For them, the night the dam broke would always be the worst night of their lives.

If you have been timed while reading this article, enter your reading time below. Then turn to the Words-per-Minute Table on page 101 and look up your reading speed (words per minute). Enter your reading speed on the graph on page 102.

Reading Time: Lesson 8

——————— : ———————
Minutes   *Seconds*

A | Finding the Main Idea

One statement below expresses the main idea of the article. One statement is too general, or too broad. The other statement explains only part of the article; it is too narrow. Label the statements using the following key:

M—Main Idea   **B—Too Broad**   **N—Too Narrow**

_____ 1. Many victims of the St. Francis Dam collapse were never found because they washed out to sea.

_____ 2. The collapse of the St. Francis Dam in 1928 caused widespread death and destruction.

_____ 3. Many dams across the United States insure an uninterrupted supply of water to major cities.

_____ Score 15 points for a correct M answer.

_____ Score 5 points for each correct B or N answer.

_____ **Total Score:** Finding the Main Idea

B | Recalling Facts

How well do you remember the facts in the article? Put an X in the box next to the answer that correctly completes each statement about the article.

1. William Mulholland was
   ☐ a. a visitor to the dam.
   ☐ b. the dam keeper.
   ☐ c. the builder of the dam.

2. After the dam broke, water roared down
   ☐ a. toward Los Angeles.
   ☐ b. the San Francisquito Canyon.
   ☐ c. the Grand Canyon.

3. At the time the dam broke, most residents of the town were
   ☐ a. asleep.
   ☐ b. nervously waiting for its collapse.
   ☐ c. away for a holiday weekend.

4. The official death toll was
   ☐ a. 150.
   ☐ b. 450.
   ☐ c. 4,500.

5. Engineer J. David Rogers believes the dam collapsed because
   ☐ a. it was built poorly.
   ☐ b. the weather was wet and rainy that year.
   ☐ c. it was built on ancient landslide rubble.

Score 5 points for each correct answer.

_____ **Total Score:** Recalling Facts

C | Making Inferences

When you combine your own experience with information from a text to draw a conclusion that is not directly stated in that text, you are making an inference. Below are five statements that may or may not be inferences based on information in the article. Label the statements using the following key:

C—Correct Inference   **F—Faulty Inference**

_____ 1. Large cities such as Los Angeles need a reliable source of water.

_____ 2. Scientists can determine what has happened to a particular area in past ages by studying the land today.

_____ 3. The water that a dam holds back puts great pressure on the dam's walls.

_____ 4. Dams should not be built because they are too dangerous.

_____ 5. Builders should study an area thoroughly before building any large structures there.

Score 5 points for each correct answer.

_____ **Total Score:** Making Inferences

D | Using Words Precisely

Each numbered sentence below contains an underlined word or phrase from the article. Following the sentence are three definitions. One definition is closest to the meaning of the underlined word. One definition is opposite or nearly opposite. Label those two definitions using the following key; do not label the remaining definition.

C—Closest   **O—Opposite or Nearly Opposite**

1. Mulholland inspected the dam. He pronounced it <u>sound</u>.

_____ a. in good condition

_____ b. official

_____ c. defective

2. First one side <u>collapsed</u>.

_____ a. flew

_____ b. caved in; fell down

_____ c. rose; grew taller

3. Then, out of the darkness, an arm reached out and <u>seized</u> him.

_____ a. released

_____ b. grabbed

_____ c. struck

4. He was supposed to have built an "<u>impregnable</u>" masterpiece.

_____ a. beautiful

_____ b. weak

_____ c. strong; secure

5. He was the one who had used aqueducts and dams to bring water to <u>parched</u> Los Angeles.

_____ a. dry; thirsty

_____ b. distant

_____ c. water-filled; flooded

_____ Score 3 points for each correct C answer.

_____ Score 2 points for each correct O answer.

_____ **Total Score:** Using Words Precisely

Enter the four total scores in the spaces below, and add them together to find your Reading Comprehension Score. Then record your score on the graph on page 103.

Score	Question Type	Lesson 8
_____	Finding the Main Idea	
_____	Recalling Facts	
_____	Making Inferences	
_____	Using Words Precisely	
_____	**Reading Comprehension Score**	

Author's Approach

Put an X in the box next to the correct answer.

1. What is the authors' purpose in writing "The Night the Dam Let Go"?

☐ a. to encourage readers to check on the safety of dams in their areas

☐ b. to show that the St. Francis Dam disaster was caused by William Mulholland

☐ c. to describe a situation in which hundreds of people died suddenly and without warning

2. Judging by statements from the article, you can conclude that the authors want the reader to think that

☐ a. no one in authority truly believed the dam was dangerous.

☐ b. many officials had been very worried about the condition of the dam before it collapsed.

☐ c. the collapse of the dam was definitely Mulholland's fault.

3. Many people blamed William Mulholland for the dam collapse. Choose the statement below that best explains how the authors address the opposing point of view in the article.

☐ a. The authors state that a few people predicted that the St. Francis Dam was about to give way.

☐ b. The authors point out that the St. Francis Dam supplied much-needed water to the Los Angeles area.

☐ c. The authors report that at least one engineer believes that the dam collapsed because it had been built on ancient rubble, a fact unknown to Mulholland.

_____ Number of correct answers

Record your personal assessment of your work on the Critical Thinking Chart on page 104.

CRITICAL THINKING

81

Summarizing and Paraphrasing

Put an X in the box next to the correct answer for question 1. Follow the directions provided for question 2.

1. Below are summaries of the article. Choose the summary that says all the most important things about the article but in the fewest words.

☐ a. At least 450 people died when the St. Francis Dam collapsed on the night of March 12, 1928. The dam, built to supply water to Los Angeles, had been built by William Mulholland. He was blamed for the collapse, but it may not have been all his fault.

☐ b. At least 1,200 ranch houses in the San Francisquito Canyon were swept away by the collapse of the dam. In addition, more than 450 people lost their lives in the tragedy.

☐ c. The St. Francis Dam had been showing dangerous signs for a while when its builder, William Mulholland, assured everyone it was safe. When visitor Bill Riley stopped at the dam the day before it collapsed, he realized the dam was about to break and took his family away from it as quickly as possible. Most people were asleep when the dam actually let go at 11:57 P.M.

2. Reread paragraph 16 in the article. Below, write a summary of the paragraph in no more than 25 words.

_____

_____

_____

_____

Reread your summary and decide whether it covers the important ideas in the paragraph. Next, decide how to shorten the summary to 15 words or less without leaving out any essential information. Write this summary below.

_____

_____

_____

_____ Number of correct answers

Record your personal assessment of your work on the Critical Thinking Chart on page 104.

Critical Thinking

Put an X in the box next to the correct answer for questions 1 and 4. Follow the directions provided for the other questions.

1. From the information in paragraph 18, you can predict that the next time a dam is built,

☐ a. engineers will check for the rubble of ancient landslides on the planned site.

☐ b. engineers won't bother to check the site thoroughly because it takes too long and costs too much.

☐ c. people will check the dam regularly for signs of weakness.

2. Choose from the letters below to correctly complete the following statement. Write the letters on the lines.

In the article, _____ and _____ were alike.

a. the fate of C. H. Hunick

b. the fate of Ann Holzcloth

c. the fate of Ann Holzcloth's infant son

3. Choose from the letters below to correctly complete the following statement. Write the letters on the lines.

According to the article, _____ caused the rubble to

_____, and the effect was _____.

a. that the dam collapsed

b. the weight of the dam

c. shift

4. How is the collapse of the St. Francis Dam related to the theme of *Total Panic*?

☐ a. Some victims had to hold onto passing debris in order to survive the raging waters.

☐ b. Terrified victims of the flood ran away from the raging waters as fast as they could; many died in fear.

☐ c. The dam might have been saved if the builder had taken some danger signs more seriously.

5. In which paragraph did you find your information or details to

answer question 3? _____

_____ Number of correct answers

Record your personal assessment of your work on the Critical Thinking Chart on page 104.

Personal Response

Begin the first few sentences of your own article about a disaster such as the collapse of a dam near your home. It may tell of a real experience or one that is imagined.

_____

_____

_____

_____

Self-Assessment

From reading this article, I have learned _____

_____

_____

_____

Flood in Mozambique

They never saw it coming. "The water came so quickly," said one woman. "We were running, there was no time to get anything but the chicken. It was coming higher in a great rush, and all we could do was climb a tree."

2   In February 2000 a huge tropical storm hit the African nation of Mozambique. Heavy rain caused rivers to pour over their banks. Dams overflowed. The Limpopo River had been little more than a trickle. Suddenly it was two miles wide.

When floodwater covered their homes, many frightened families ran up to rooftops or climbed into the upper branches of tall trees. For days they clung to their uncomfortable perches waiting for rescue.

The flood swept up homes, even whole villages. Hundreds of people drowned. Nearly a million were left homeless. "It's like the gods have abandoned us," said one man. "We can't believe this is happening to our country."

3   The woman with the chicken was among the lucky ones. When the flood hit her village, some people panicked and just ran. But she climbed a tree with her 6-month-old baby strapped to her back. Some of her neighbors did the same. As they clung to the branches, they watched the brown floodwater of the Limpopo River raging below them. "I saw people drowning," said the woman. "We were relieved to [get] to the tree. But it was scary with all the insects and no food or sleep. I only held on because of my baby."

4   Holding on wasn't easy. If any of the people in the trees fell asleep, they might fall out and drown. None of them had more to eat than a piece of bread or an ear of corn. Some had nothing at all. As the hours passed, their hunger grew. So did their weariness. But still they hung on. Hour after hour, day after day, they clung to the trees and prayed that rescuers would come.

5   During the day the temperature often rose to 100 degrees or more. But the nights were even worse. That was when the mosquitoes came out. Also, other creatures had fled to the trees to escape the flood. So people had to share their haven with stinging ants, rats, and snakes. "It was like another world—just the water beneath us and the sky above," said one woman.

6   Even before the flood hit, the people in Mozambique had difficult lives. They are among the poorest people in the world. The average person makes less than $150 per year. That is why the woman bothered to take the chicken. It was her sole possession. The other villagers were just as poor. Because they had no radios, they got no warning about the flood. Also, none of these people had cars or trucks. They couldn't drive to higher and drier land. The woman who took the chicken had never been inside a car. So when the floodwater came, the people's only hope was to climb a tall tree or a rooftop.

7   But in a poor country devastated by floodwater, who was left to rescue survivors? Mozambique did not have

the skilled people and equipment to help the victims. "We cannot do this alone," said the president. "The damage is massive and we need help fast."

8   Yet other countries acted slowly. Perhaps they did not know how bad the flood really was. In any case, the only nation that rushed to help was South Africa. That country, too, had been hit by the flood, but not as badly. It sent 12 helicopters to lift people out of trees and off rooftops.

9   It was tough work. The flooded area was vast and it was hard to see people in the trees. Often, pilots had to use the wind caused by the helicopters' blades to flatten out tree leaves a bit. Only then could pilots see if there were people in a tree to rescue. The pilots flew day after day with little sleep. They did this for more than two weeks. In the end, they saved nearly 14,000 people. "They are the real heroes," said one official.

10   Of all the survivors, it was Sophia Pedro whose story captured the world's attention. Like so many others, she and her family are poor. All they owned were 10 pigs and 10 chickens. They lived in a grass hut in a rural village. "We did not have [the] money for bricks," said her husband.

11   Sophia was nine months pregnant when the flood hit. She, her husband, and their two children were at home at the time. The water rose so fast they barely got out in time. They fled with just the clothes on their backs. Luckily they managed to scramble up into a tree. But they hadn't had time to take any food with them. So they had nothing to eat. The only water they had to drink was the muddy water below. For four days they stayed in the tree, clinging to life.

12   Then, on the fourth day, two miracles occurred. First, Sophia gave birth to a baby girl. Somehow, she managed to hang onto a branch during her labor pains. Second, the family was saved by a helicopter. Moments after the baby's birth, a medic was lowered down to the tree. There he cut the baby's cord and comforted Sophia. "We spotted her just in time," he said. "We then hoisted mother and child onto the helicopter." The drama was caught by a TV crew and broadcast around the world. Many people saw the birth as a ray of hope in a sea of misery.

13   Despite their ordeal, Sophia and her baby, named Rositha, were in good shape. "We are very happy to have been rescued," she said. "We have no problem."

14   But what kind of future would Rositha have? After the rescue, her father said, "We have nothing. We had our last meal four days ago. Our village is all gone."

15   Soon the leader of Mozambique stepped in to help. The president promised that the family would get a better place to live and food to eat. He also said the government would pay for Rositha's schooling. The president said the girl was a symbol of the suffering of all children in the nation. So although Rositha's life started on a shaky note, it seemed she would have a decent chance for a good life.

If you have been timed while reading this article, enter your reading time below. Then turn to the Words-per-Minute Table on page 101 and look up your reading speed (words per minute). Enter your reading speed on the graph on page 102.

Reading Time: Lesson 9

_____ : _____
Minutes   *Seconds*

A | Finding the Main Idea

One statement below expresses the main idea of the article. One statement is too general, or too broad. The other statement explains only part of the article; it is too narrow. Label the statements using the following key:

M—Main Idea   **B—Too Broad**   **N—Too Narrow**

_____ 1. Sophia Pedro and her family attracted worldwide attention during the February 2000 flood in Mozambique when Sophia gave birth in a tree.

_____ 2. Floods cause death and incredible damage.

_____ 3. A terrible flood caused by a tropical storm hit the nation of Mozambique in February 2000, killing hundreds of people and leaving millions homeless.

_____ Score 15 points for a correct M answer.

_____ Score 5 points for each correct B or N answer.

_____ **Total Score:** Finding the Main Idea

B | Recalling Facts

How well do you remember the facts in the article? Put an X in the box next to the answer that correctly completes each statement about the article.

1. Mozambique is a nation in
   □ a. Africa.
   □ b. Asia.
   □ c. Europe.

2. At the time of the flood, the average person in Mozambique earned about
   □ a. $15,000 per year.
   □ b. $1,500 per year.
   □ c. $150 per year.

3. To escape the flood, most people
   □ a. drove their cars to higher, drier ground.
   □ b. climbed to the tops of tall trees or roofs.
   □ c. took the train to an area that was not flooded.

4. The only nation that rushed to help the flood victims in Mozambique was
   □ a. the United States.
   □ b. Russia.
   □ c. South Africa.

5. Rositha Pedro was born
   □ a. on a rooftop.
   □ b. in a tree.
   □ c. in a helicopter.

Score 5 points for each correct answer.

_____ **Total Score:** Recalling Facts

C **Making Inferences**

When you combine your own experience with information from a text to draw a conclusion that is not directly stated in that text, you are making an inference. Below are five statements that may or may not be inferences based on information in the article. Label the statements using the following key:

C—Correct Inference   **F—Faulty Inference**

_____ 1. Warnings about the flood were probably announced on the radio.

_____ 2. The lives of all the people of Mozambique improved after the flood.

_____ 3. Raising a chicken doesn't cost a great deal of money.

_____ 4. When there is trouble anywhere in the world, people can count on the United States to be the first to help.

_____ 5. In February the trees in Mozambique are bare and leafless.

Score 5 points for each correct answer.

_____ **Total Score:** Making Inferences

 D **Using Words Precisely**

Each numbered sentence below contains an underlined word or phrase from the article. Following the sentence are three definitions. One definition is closest to the meaning of the underlined word. One definition is opposite or nearly opposite. Label those two definitions using the following key; do not label the remaining definition.

C—Closest   **O—Opposite or Nearly Opposite**

1. So people had to share their <u>haven</u> with stinging ants, rats, and snakes.

_____ a. place of safety

_____ b. dangerous place

_____ c. tree

2. It was her <u>sole</u> possession.

_____ a. favorite

_____ b. only

_____ c. one of many

3. But in a poor country <u>devastated</u> by floodwater, who was left to rescue survivors?

_____ a. improved

_____ b. changed

_____ c. ruined

4. They lived in a grass hut in a <u>rural</u> village.

_____ a. country

_____ b. big city

_____ c. friendly

5. Despite their <u>ordeal</u>, Sophia and her baby, named Rositha, were in good shape.

_____ a. pleasant experience

_____ b. complaining

_____ c. suffering

_____ Score 3 points for each correct C answer.

_____ Score 2 points for each correct O answer.

_____ **Total Score:** Using Words Precisely

Enter the four total scores in the spaces below, and add them together to find your Reading Comprehension Score. Then record your score on the graph on page 103.

Score	Question Type	Lesson 9
_____	Finding the Main Idea	
_____	Recalling Facts	
_____	Making Inferences	
_____	Using Words Precisely	
_____	**Reading Comprehension Score**	

Author's Approach

Put an X in the box next to the correct answer.

1. What is the authors' purpose in writing "Flood in Mozambique"?

☐ a. to encourage the reader to give money to international rescue efforts

☐ b. to inform the reader about a huge flood and the efforts of its victims to survive

☐ c. to express an opinion about cooperation between countries

2. Which of the following statements from the article best describes the wealth of most of the people of Mozambique?

☐ a. Mozambique did not have the skilled people and equipment to help the victims.

☐ b. So people had to share their haven with stinging ants, rats, and snakes.

☐ c. They were among the poorest people in the world.

3. What do the authors imply by saying "So although Rositha's life started on a shaky note, it seemed she would have a decent chance for a good life"?

☐ a. No one can be sure whether Rositha will have a good life or a difficult life.

☐ b. Rositha is sure to have much wealth throughout her life.

☐ c. Rositha will probably have more opportunities than many people in her country.

_____ Number of correct answers

Record your personal assessment of your work on the Critical Thinking Chart on page 104.

Summarizing and Paraphrasing

Follow the directions provided for question 1. Put an X in the box next to the correct answer for question 2.

1. Look for the important ideas and events in paragraphs 4 and 5. Summarize those paragraphs in one or two sentences.

_____

_____

_____

_____

2. Choose the sentence that correctly restates the following sentence from the article "As they clung to the branches, they watched the brown floodwater of the Limpopo River raging below them."

☐ a. The Limpopo River's brown floodwater reached the branches of the trees that the people had climbed.

☐ b. The people holding onto the tree branches could see the wild, brown Limpopo River below them.

☐ c. Below, in the Limpopo River, the people could see the tree branches swirling.

_____ Number of correct answers

Record your personal assessment of your work on the Critical Thinking Chart on page 104.

Critical Thinking

Follow the directions provided for questions 1, 3, 4, and 5. Put an X in the box next to the correct answer for question 2.

1. For each statement below, write *O* if it expresses an opinion or write *F* if it expresses a fact.

_____ a. If the TV crew hadn't reported Sophia Pedro's story, the president of Mozambique might not have promised her and her family a better place to live and food to eat.

_____ b. Sophia Pedro and her family deserved more help than any other family in Mozambique.

_____ c. Helicopter pilots saved nearly 14,000 flood victims.

2. From what Sophia Pedro said, you can predict that she will

☐ a. complain if she doesn't get a great deal of special attention for years to come.

☐ b. be happy with any help her family will receive.

☐ c. criticize the government for not rescuing her and her family sooner.

3. Choose from the letters below to correctly complete the following statement. Write the letters on the lines.

In the article, _____ and _____ are different.

a. Europe's response to the emergency in Mozambique

b. South Africa's response to the emergency in Mozambique

c. North America's response to the emergency in Mozambique

4. Think about cause-effect relationships in the article. Fill in the blanks in the cause-effect chart, drawing from the letters below.

Cause	Effect
A tropical storm with heavy rain struck Mozambique.	_____
Most people in Mozambique had no radios.	_____
_____	The Pedro family lived in a grass hut.

a. The Limpopo River overflowed its banks.

b. They couldn't afford a brick house.

c. They did not hear warnings about the coming flood.

5. Which paragraphs from the article provide evidence that supports your answer to question 4? _____

_____ Number of correct answers

Record your personal assessment of your work on the Critical Thinking Chart on page 104.

Personal Response

I can't believe _____

_____

_____

_____

_____

Self-Assessment

I was confused on question _____ in the _____ section because _____

_____

_____

_____

_____

Tragedy in the Baltic Sea

Finnish military personnel load the coffin of a shipwreck victim onto a ferryboat on the Baltic Sea. The calm waters give no hint of the violence of the storm that struck only days earlier. This victim and 858 others lost their lives when the ferry Estonia sank during a storm.

It was just after midnight on the ferryboat *Estonia*. Andrus Maidre awoke with a start. From below his cabin came loud crashing sounds. Dozens of cars and trucks were sliding back and forth, smashing into each other. As 19-year-old Maidre crawled up the tilting stairway to the upper deck, he realized what was happening. The ferryboat was sinking.

2   The *Estonia* was a popular ship. It was known for its restaurants and shops. It had an indoor swimming pool and a children's playroom. And it had a live band for dancing. In short, sailing on the *Estonia* was a fun way to cross the Baltic Sea.

3   On September 27, 1994, the ship sailed from Tallinn, Estonia. It was headed for Stockholm, Sweden. There were 996 people on board. Many were Swedish tourists. For them, the 230-mile trip was a pleasure cruise. The forecast called for high winds and rough seas. But no one seemed worried. Such conditions were normal at that time of the year. Besides, the *Estonia* was a big ship. It was more than 500 feet long and weighed more than 15,000 tons. It looked as though it could handle any kind of bad weather that came its way.

4   By 8:30 that night, the Baltic Sea had turned nasty. Twenty-foot waves battered the ferry. The ship rolled from side to side. The band decided to call it quits early. The sea was getting too rough for dancing. Most of the passengers went to their cabins. By midnight, almost everyone was asleep. Up to that point, it had been just a very turbulent night.

5   But then things turned deadly. The storm grew really violent, with waves swelling to more than 30 feet high. Somehow, the front cargo door became ripped open. At 12:10 A.M., a member of the crew glanced up at his TV monitor. He noticed water in the car deck. He thought it was rain coming in. So he ordered the bilge pumps turned on.

6   But the pumps did no good. The water was not simply the result of rain. The sea itself was pouring into the car deck through the broken cargo door. Tons of water sloshed from side to side in the car deck. The crew soon realized what was happening. But there was little they could do. By 12:24 A.M., they knew all hope was lost. The message went out: "Mayday, *Estonia*. We are sinking."

7   By that time, the ship was leaning sharply to the left. Cars and trucks began to bang into each other. As the noise woke the passengers, fear and confusion swept through the ship. People rushed around, screaming for help. Some wore only their pajamas. Others wore nothing. Carl Ovberg later recalled what he saw. "Children and women were running in panic," he said. "Many fell and slid headlong into the walls. You couldn't help them. The boat was swinging and you could hardly manage to stay on your own feet."

8   Andrus Maidre said, "Some old people had already given up hope. They were just sitting there crying." Maidre added, "I also stepped over children who were wailing and holding on to the railing."

9　The *Estonia* had plenty of life rafts. And it had all the life jackets people needed. But the safety equipment did little good. The ship sank too fast for an orderly rescue. In just 35 minutes, it was gone. For the most part, passengers had to look out for themselves. There was no attempt to save the women and children first. "It was the law of the jungle," said Kent Härstedt. "A woman had broken her legs and begged others to give her a life jacket." No one did.

10　But there was some heroism too. One group of Swedes formed a human chain. They threw life jackets to people who had fallen into the sea without one. One man jumped into the water. He swam to one of the life rafts and climbed aboard. Struggling bravely, he pulled others up onto the raft. But, sadly, not everyone made it. "There was an Estonian girl," he later recalled. "I tried to hold on to her, but my fingers were so stiff. She went down into the water when a big wave came over the [raft]."

11　Many passengers remained trapped deep inside the ship. Some of them woke up too late to get out. Others left their cabins in time but couldn't reach the upper deck. That was especially true for women, children, and older people. One investigator later explained why.

"Getting up from the lower decks was very difficult," he said. "Passengers were faced with stairs that were upside down. The only way of climbing them would have been to hang monkey like from the railings. That requires strength."

12　Some of those who did get off the ship died anyway. The water was frigid. Once in the sea, many people perished from shock and exposure. Only those lucky enough to reach a life raft had any real chance. That was how one man survived. "I grabbed a life jacket," he said, "and then the [ferry] fell on its left side completely. I managed to jump into a rubber boat with three other people."

13　The first rescue ship arrived at 3:35 A.M. It was the Finnish ferry *Mariella*. Its captain was Jan Thure Törnroos. The night was dark, but Törnroos could see with the help of searchlights. It was a grim sight. "We could see people floating about in the water and hear them screaming for help," he said. "There were hundreds of bodies bobbing up and down."

14　Rescuing those who were still alive was not easy. The sea was very rough. Helicopters had to pull most of the people out of the water. The rescue effort went on for seven hours. Some people died waiting. Paul Barney made it to a raft with 11 other people. But icy waves kept breaking over their raft. Six of them died from the cold. "Every time we got slightly warmer," Barney said, "we got drenched again."

15　In all, 859 people died. Of those, 765 went down with the ship. The *Estonia* became their tomb. Another 94 died after jumping from the ferry. In the end, just 137 people survived. Of those, only 26 were women and only 23 were younger than 18. The loss of the *Estonia* was one of the worst ferry disasters of all time. Prime Minister Carl Bildt of Sweden summed up everyone's feelings. It was, he said "a human tragedy beyond belief." And so it was.

If you have been timed while reading this article, enter your reading time below. Then turn to the Words-per-Minute Table on page 101 and look up your reading speed (words per minute). Enter your reading speed on the graph on page 102.

Reading Time: Lesson 10

_____ : _____
Minutes　　*Seconds*

A | Finding the Main Idea

One statement below expresses the main idea of the article. One statement is too general, or too broad. The other statement explains only part of the article; it is too narrow. Label the statements using the following key:

M—Main Idea   **B—Too Broad**   **N—Too Narrow**

_____ 1. When water entered the cargo area of the ferry *Estonia* in stormy waters, the ferry turned over and sank within 35 minutes, killing 859 people.

_____ 2. Despite careful construction and management, ships are still at risk from bad weather and heavy seas, as the disaster of the ferry *Estonia* proved.

_____ 3. When the ferry *Estonia* sailed from Tallinn, Estonia, bound for Stockholm, Sweden, it carried 996 people.

_____ Score 15 points for a correct M answer.

_____ Score 5 points for each correct B or N answer.

_____ **Total Score:** Finding the Main Idea

B | Recalling Facts

How well do you remember the facts in the article? Put an X in the box next to the answer that correctly completes each statement about the article.

1. The *Estonia* was crossing the Baltic Sea between Tallinn, Estonia, and
☐ a. St. Petersburg, Russia.
☐ b. Oslo, Norway.
☐ c. Stockholm, Sweden.

2. At 12:10 A.M., a TV monitor showed water
☐ a. entering passengers' cabins.
☐ b. inside the car deck.
☐ c. coming over the top deck.

3. Water entering the lower decks made the ferry
☐ a. stop moving.
☐ b. drop straight down.
☐ c. lean sharply to one side.

4. Few passengers got into life rafts because
☐ a. the ship went down so fast.
☐ b. there were not enough life rafts.
☐ c. the crew took all the life rafts.

5. Many of the people who jumped from the ferry
☐ a. were saved by rescue ships after 12 hours in the water.
☐ b. died of exposure and shock.
☐ c. were elderly.

Score 5 points for each correct answer.

_____ **Total Score:** Recalling Facts

C Making Inferences

When you combine your own experience with information from a text to draw a conclusion that is not directly stated in that text, you are making an inference. Below are five statements that may or may not be inferences based on information in the article. Label the statements using the following key:

C—Correct Inference   **F—Faulty Inference**

_____ 1. Ferries with designs similar to that of the *Estonia* are never safe in rough waters.

_____ 2. The weak point of the *Estonia* was its cargo door design.

_____ 3. If the crew had sounded alarms and awakened all the passengers, hundreds more of the people on the *Estonia* would have been saved.

_____ 4. When a ship sinks as fast as the *Estonia* did, the passengers with the best chance of survival are men between 20 and 50 years old.

_____ 5. People who survive a disaster, such as the sinking of the *Estonia*, may later regret their own actions during the event.

Score 5 points for each correct answer.

_____ **Total Score:** Making Inferences

D Using Words Precisely

Each numbered sentence below contains an underlined word or phrase from the article. Following the sentence are three definitions. One definition is closest to the meaning of the underlined word. One definition is opposite or nearly opposite. Label those two definitions using the following key; do not label the remaining definition.

C—Closest   **O—Opposite or Nearly Opposite**

1. Twenty-foot waves <u>battered</u> the ferry.

_____ a. rose above

_____ b. protected

_____ c. pounded

2. Up to that point, it had been just a very <u>turbulent</u> night.

_____ a. peaceful; smooth

_____ b. stormy; rough

_____ c. annoying

3. The storm grew really violent, with waves <u>swelling</u> to more than 30 feet.

_____ a. growing

_____ b. shrinking

_____ c. crashing

4. Tons of water <u>sloshed</u> from side to side in the car deck.

_____ a. caused damage

_____ b. splashed about

_____ c. sat calmly

5. Some of those who did get off the ship died anyway. The water was <u>frigid</u>.

_____ a. freezing

_____ b. moving violently

_____ c. warm

_____ Score 3 points for each correct C answer.

_____ Score 2 points for each correct O answer.

_____ **Total Score:** Using Words Precisely

Enter the four total scores in the spaces below, and add them together to find your Reading Comprehension Score. Then record your score on the graph on page 103.

Score	Question Type	Lesson 10
_____	Finding the Main Idea	
_____	Recalling Facts	
_____	Making Inferences	
_____	Using Words Precisely	
_____	**Reading Comprehension Score**	

Author's Approach

Put an X in the box next to the correct answer.

1. The authors use the first sentence of the article to

☐ a. describe the setting of the disaster.

☐ b. describe the personality of Andrus Maidre.

☐ c. compare ferryboats and tugboats.

2. From the statements below, choose those that you believe the authors would agree with.

☐ a. The *Estonia* did not have enough safety equipment for all its passengers.

☐ b. The ship sank too quickly for its passengers to abandon it safely.

☐ c. Many women and children died because they did not have enough strength to reach the upper deck and board life rafts.

3. The authors tell this story mainly by

☐ a. describing events in the order they happened.

☐ b. comparing different topics.

☐ c. using their imagination and creativity.

_____ Number of correct answers

Record your personal assessment of your work on the Critical Thinking Chart on page 104.

Summarizing and Paraphrasing

Follow the directions provided for questions 1 and 2. Put an X in the box next to the correct answer for question 3.

1. Look for the important ideas and events in paragraphs 5 and 6. Summarize those paragraphs in one or two sentences.

_____

_____

_____

_____

2. Complete the following one-sentence summary of the article using the lettered phrases from the phrase bank below. Write the letters on the lines.

> **Phrase Bank**
> a. events during the disaster
> b. the rescue of the survivors and a summary of the casualties
> c. a description of the *Estonia* before it sank

The article "Tragedy in the Baltic Sea" begins with _____,

goes on to explain _____, and ends with _____.

3. Read the statement from the article below. Then read the paraphrase of that statement. Choose the reason that best tells why the paraphrase does not say the same thing as the statement.

Statement: A group of Swedes helped by forming a human chain and by tossing life jackets to people who needed them.

Paraphrase: The way a group of Swedes decided to help was by throwing safety equipment to people in need.

☐ a. Paraphrase says too much.

☐ b. Paraphrase doesn't say enough.

☐ c. Paraphrase doesn't agree with the statement.

> _____ Number of correct answers
>
> Record your personal assessment of your work on the Critical Thinking Chart on page 104.

Critical Thinking

Follow the directions provided for questions 1, 3, and 4. Put an X in the box next to the correct answer for the other questions.

1. For each statement below, write *O* if it expresses an opinion or write *F* if it expresses a fact.

_____ a. The *Estonia* was reckless for setting out on such a stormy night.

_____ b. The men on the *Estonia* were selfish; they should have helped women and children more.

_____ c. The *Estonia* was sailing from Tallinn, Estonia, headed for Stockholm, Sweden.

2. From the article, you can predict that if there had been more time between the discovery that the ship was sinking and its actual sinking,

☐ a. more people would have been saved.

☐ b. fewer people would have survived.

☐ c. probably the same number would have be saved.

3. Using what you know about the sinking of the *Titanic* and what is told about the sinking of the *Estonia* in the article, name three ways the *Estonia* disaster is similar to and three ways it is different from the sinking of the *Titanic*. Cite the paragraph number(s) where you found details in the article to support your conclusions.

Similarities

_____

_____

_____

Differences

_____

_____

_____

4. Reread paragraph 11. Then choose from the letters below to correctly complete the following statement. Write the letters on the lines.

According to paragraph 11, _____ because _____.

a. many passengers were trapped inside the ship

b. some passengers left their cabins in time to reach the upper deck

c. the stairs to the upper deck had been turned upside down

5. What did you have to do to answer question 1?

☐ a. recognize a fact (something that you can prove is true)

☐ b. find a description (how something looks)

☐ c. find a cause (why something happened)

_____ Number of correct answers

Record your personal assessment of your work on the Critical Thinking Chart on page 104.

Personal Response

If I were the author, I would change _____

_____

because _____

_____

_____

Self-Assessment

I'm proud of how I answered question _____ in the _____ section because _____

_____

_____

_____

Compare and Contrast

Think about the articles you have read in Unit Two. Pick three situations that were caused not by people, but by the forces of nature. Write the titles of the articles that tell about them in the first column of the chart below. Use information you learned from the articles to fill in the empty boxes in the chart.

Title	What natural force caused this terrifying event?	How did the frightened people try to cope with the disaster?	How many people were killed or injured in this disaster?

If you could ask someone who lived through this disaster one question, what would it be? _____

_____

_____

Words-per-Minute Table

Unit Two

Directions: If you were timed while reading an article, refer to the Reading Time you recorded in the box at the end of the article. Use this Words-per-Minute Table to determine your reading speed for that article. Then plot your reading speed on the graph on page 102.

Lesson No. of Words	6 1,125	7 1,204	8 1,114	9 1,032	10 1,089	Seconds
1:30	752	803	743	688	726	90
1:40	677	722	662	619	653	100
1:50	615	657	608	563	594	110
2:00	564	602	557	516	545	120
2:10	521	556	514	476	503	130
2:20	483	516	477	442	467	140
2:30	451	482	446	413	436	150
2:40	423	452	418	387	408	160
2:50	398	425	393	364	384	170
3:00	376	401	371	344	363	180
3:10	356	380	352	326	344	190
3:20	338	361	334	310	327	200
3:30	322	344	318	295	311	210
3:40	308	328	304	281	297	220
3:50	294	314	291	269	284	230
4:00	282	301	279	258	272	240
4:10	271	289	267	248	261	250
4:20	260	278	257	238	251	260
4:30	251	268	248	229	242	270
4:40	242	258	239	221	233	280
4:50	233	249	230	214	225	290
5:00	226	241	223	206	218	300
5:10	218	233	216	200	211	310
5:20	212	226	209	194	204	320
5:30	205	219	203	188	198	330
5:40	199	212	197	182	192	340
5:50	193	206	191	177	187	350
6:00	188	201	186	172	182	360
6:10	183	195	181	167	177	370
6:20	178	190	176	163	172	380
6:30	174	185	171	159	168	390
6:40	169	181	167	155	163	400
6:50	165	176	163	151	159	410
7:00	161	172	159	147	156	420
7:10	157	168	155	144	152	430
7:20	154	164	152	141	149	440
7:30	150	161	149	138	145	450
7:40	147	157	145	135	142	460
7:50	144	154	142	132	139	470
8:00	141	151	139	129	136	480

Minutes and Seconds

Plotting Your Progress: Reading Speed

Unit Two

Directions: If you were timed while reading an article, write your words-per-minute rate for that article in the box under the number of the lesson. Then plot your reading speed on the graph by putting a small X on the line directly above the number of the lesson, across from the number of words per minute you read. As you mark your speed for each lesson, graph your progress by drawing a line to connect the X's.

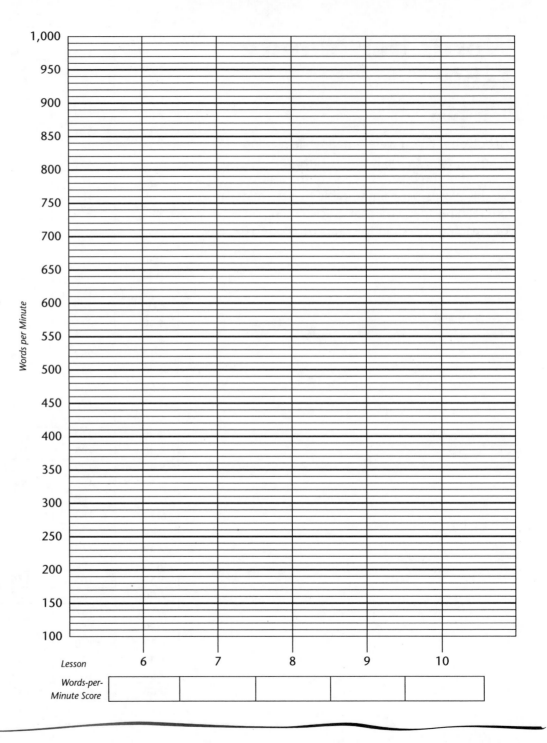

Words per Minute

1,000
950
900
850
800
750
700
650
600
550
500
450
400
350
300
250
200
150
100

Lesson   6   7   8   9   10

Words-per-Minute Score

Plotting Your Progress: Reading Comprehension

Unit Two

Directions: Write your Reading Comprehension Score for each lesson in the box under the number of the lesson. Then plot your score on the graph by putting a small X on the line directly above the number of the lesson and across from the score you earned. As you mark your score for each lesson, graph your progress by drawing a line to connect the X's.

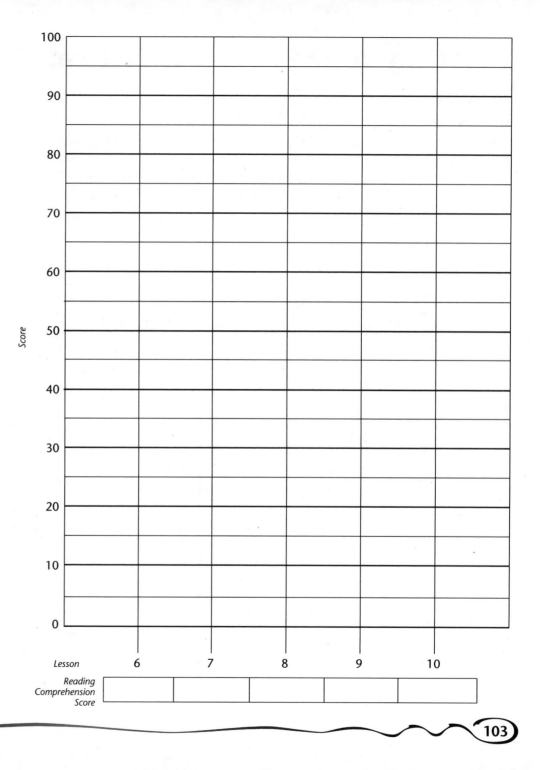

Lesson	6	7	8	9	10
Reading Comprehension Score					

Plotting Your Progress: Critical Thinking

Unit Two

Directions: Work with your teacher to evaluate your responses to the Critical Thinking questions for each lesson. Then fill in the appropriate spaces in the chart below. For each lesson and each type of Critical Thinking question, do the following: Mark a minus sign (–) in the box to indicate areas in which you feel you could improve. Mark a plus sign (+) to indicate areas in which you feel you did well. Mark a minus-slash-plus sign (–/+) to indicate areas in which you had mixed success. Then write any comments you have about your performance, including ideas for improvement.

Lesson	Author's Approach	Summarizing and Paraphrasing	Critical Thinking
6			
7			
8			
9			
10			

UNIT THREE

A Horrible Way to Die

Thirty-six-year-old Kimfumu had a fever. His head ached. And he had diarrhea. So in early April of 1995, Kimfumu went to the main hospital in Kikwit, Zaire (present-day Democratic Republic of the Congo). Doctors thought he had an infection in his intestines. They treated him for it, but over the next two days he grew worse. At last, doctors chose to operate. They hoped to fix whatever was wrong inside Kimfumu's belly.

2   The operation turned into a nightmare. When doctors opened Kimfumu up, they found his insides

This is no ordinary funeral. The pallbearers are medical personnel protected by masks, gowns, and gloves against an invisible killer. That killer is the dreaded Ebola virus. Who will be its next victim?

were dissolving. His organs were literally turning to mush. There was nothing doctors could do to help him. They sewed him back up and tried to ease his pain. A nun named Sister Floralba took over his care. She knew about his condition. In fact, she had been present during the operation. As Sister Floralba watched in horror, blood began to pour from Kimfumu's nose. His ears and even his eyes began to bleed. On April 14, Kimfumu died.

3   By then, Sister Floralba herself was feeling ill. She, too, developed a fever. She, too, had a headache and diarrhea. Three of her friends, all of them nuns, did what they could. They drove Sister Floralba 50 miles to a bigger hospital. But within days, she died the same horrifying death as Kimfumu had.

4   The next day, Sister Floralba's three friends became sick. One by one, they all died. By then, doctors realized what was happening. Some terrible disease was spreading through Kikwit. Each day, new cases came in. Victims all showed the same hideous symptoms. A few survived. But most were dying.

5   Doctors took blood samples from some of the victims. They rushed the

samples to the United States. Doctors at the Centers for Disease Control (CDC) in Atlanta, Georgia, studied the samples. On May 11, CDC doctors announced their findings. They had figured out what was causing the deaths in Kikwit. It was the dreaded Ebola virus.

6   Ebola was first identified in 1976. At that time, it killed about 400 people in another part of Zaire. Doctors knew the virus was deadly. They knew it spread through contact with a victim's blood. But they didn't know how the virus got into human blood in the first place. Dr. Peter Piot was one of the doctors who discovered Ebola. As he said in 1995, "Where Ebola comes from is a very big question mark."

7   Many doctors, including Dr. Piot, think Ebola comes from deep within Africa's rain forests. It may live in the body of some rodent or insect there. The virus probably does not harm this "host" creature. As long as the host has no contact with human beings, everything is fine. But now people are cutting down rain forests. So hosts and humans are meeting. As they do, the virus has a chance to enter the human body. And while

the virus does not hurt the host, it is deadly to humans.

8   After the 1976 outbreak, the virus faded back into the rain forest. But then, in 1995, it had returned. By the time Sister Floralba's three friends died, terror filled the streets of Kikwit. Few people knew exactly what was happening. But they saw that death was all around them. By mid-May, 77 people had died. Each day, that number climbed higher.

9   Doctors from around the world rushed to Kikwit to help. A horrendous mess awaited them. The hospital where Kimfumu died was filthy. "People were vomiting," said one U.S. doctor. "There was . . . blood all over the floors and walls. The dead were lying among the living." There were no masks, no gowns, no clean instruments. Given the conditions, it was easy to see how virus-filled blood had spread from one person to the next.

10   There was another problem as well. By the time outside doctors arrived, many patients and staff members had fled in fear. That raised a chilling question. Were these runaways spreading the disease to other places? Would Ebola soon break out in bigger cities? Would it become a worldwide plague?

11   For days, people everywhere held their breath. It could take the virus up to 21 days to produce symptoms in a victim. So no one knew just how far it had spread. The government of Zaire closed all the schools in Kikwit. Medical clinics were also closed. Officials ordered people to stay in their homes. Still, every day, more and more cases were reported.

12   Meanwhile, medical teams fanned out to nearby villages. They tried to explain the danger to people there. They begged villagers to treat their sick carefully. They pleaded with families to refrain from normal burial customs. Those customs involved handling the bloody organs of the dead person. If family members insisted on a normal burial, doctors urged them to wear rubber gloves.

13   Some people tried to do what the medical teams said. Others simply threw up their hands. "It's useless for us to do anything," said one villager. "What can we do against this disease?" Still others heard the news too late. A man named Mola had just finished burying his father when a medical team found him. "I don't know what to say," said Mola. "I am the one who helped [my father]. I have already touched the body. And now you tell me I must avoid contact?"

14   By May 26, 121 people had died of Ebola. Three weeks later, the number was up to 220. By July, it had gone to 315.

But then—luckily—the virus died out. All the people who had been exposed to Ebola had either died or fought it off. By August 24, the epidemic was over.

15   Officials believe the Ebola virus still lurks in Africa's rain forests. It is there, hiding, in some host creature. We don't know what that host is. And we don't know when, if ever, Ebola will try to leap back into human bodies. But the threat of Ebola is a real one. It is one more reason why we should think twice before cutting down the world's remaining rain forests.

A | Finding the Main Idea

One statement below expresses the main idea of the article. One statement is too general, or too broad. The other statement explains only part of the article; it is too narrow. Label the statements using the following key:

M—Main Idea   **B—Too Broad**   **N—Too Narrow**

_____ 1. The Ebola virus caused one of the most dangerous and mysterious diseases to appear in years.

_____ 2. Doctors who operated on the first of the Ebola virus's victims, Kimfumu, discovered that his organs were dissolving.

_____ 3. The Ebola virus that struck Kikwit in 1995 killed hundreds and left Africans in fear that it could strike again.

_____ Score 15 points for a correct M answer.

_____ Score 5 points for each correct B or N answer.

_____ **Total Score:** Finding the Main Idea

B | Recalling Facts

How well do you remember the facts in the article? Put an X in the box next to the answer that correctly completes each statement about the article.

1. Kimfumu's symptoms included
   - ☐ a. fever and diarrhea.
   - ☐ b. dizziness and loss of memory.
   - ☐ c. loss of the use of his legs.

2. Doctors rushed blood samples to the Centers for Disease Control in
   - ☐ a. Cairo, Egypt.
   - ☐ b. New York City.
   - ☐ c. Atlanta, Georgia.

3. Some doctors believe the Ebola virus comes from
   - ☐ a. improperly cooked meat.
   - ☐ b. an insect or rodent in the rain forest.
   - ☐ c. worms in garbage.

4. The Ebola virus is spread through
   - ☐ a. contact with a victim's blood.
   - ☐ b. coughs and sneezes.
   - ☐ c. mosquito bites.

5. For the families of Ebola victims, the most dangerous part of traditional burial customs is
   - ☐ a. taking the victim into the rain forest.
   - ☐ b. handling the victim's bloody organs.
   - ☐ c. slowly drying out the victim's body.

Score 5 points for each correct answer.

_____ **Total Score:** Recalling Facts

C Making Inferences

When you combine your own experience with information from a text to draw a conclusion that is not directly stated in that text, you are making an inference. Below are five statements that may or may not be inferences based on information in the article. Label the statements using the following key:

C—Correct Inference   **F—Faulty Inference**

_____ 1. The Ebola virus kills its victims quickly.

_____ 2. Doctors believe that viruses cannot travel through the rubber in rubber gloves.

_____ 3. The rain forest is a dangerous breeding ground for viruses and should be destroyed.

_____ 4. We now know that the Ebola virus is a danger only in Kikwit.

_____ 5. Since the Ebola virus is found in Africa's rain forests, we can be sure it also lives in the rain forests of South America and Asia.

Score 5 points for each correct answer.

_____ **Total Score:** Making Inferences

D Using Words Precisely

Each numbered sentence below contains an underlined word or phrase from the article. Following the sentence are three definitions. One definition is closest to the meaning of the underlined word. One definition is opposite or nearly opposite. Label those two definitions using the following key; do not label the remaining definition.

C—Closest   **O—Opposite or Nearly Opposite**

1. But within days, she died the same <u>horrifying</u> death as Kimfumu had.

_____ a. frightening

_____ b. natural

_____ c. comforting

2. Victims all showed the same <u>hideous</u> symptoms.

_____ a. lovely

_____ b. ugly

_____ c. secret

3. A <u>horrendous</u> mess awaited them.

_____ a. amazing

_____ b. terrible; nasty

_____ c. pleasant

4. Meanwhile, medical teams <u>fanned out</u> to nearby villages.

_____ a. drew together

_____ b. sent messages

_____ c. spread out

5. They pleaded with families to <u>refrain from</u> normal burial customs.

_____ a. skip

_____ b. continue with

_____ c. recall

_____ Score 3 points for each correct C answer.

_____ Score 2 points for each correct O answer.

_____ **Total Score:** Using Words Precisely

Enter the four total scores in the spaces below, and add them together to find your Reading Comprehension Score. Then record your score on the graph on page 149.

Score	Question Type	Lesson 11
_____	Finding the Main Idea	
_____	Recalling Facts	
_____	Making Inferences	
_____	Using Words Precisely	
_____	**Reading Comprehension Score**	

Author's Approach

Put an X in the box next to the correct answer.

1. What is the authors' purpose in writing "A Horrible Way to Die"?

☐ a. to encourage readers to become doctors

☐ b. to inform readers about a frightening disease that struck Zaire

☐ c. to express an opinion about medical care in Zaire

2. From the statements below, choose those that you believe the authors would agree with.

☐ a. Zaire officials never took the Ebola danger seriously.

☐ b. People should stop cutting down rain forests.

☐ c. Zaire doctors welcomed the help that doctors from other countries could give them.

3. Judging by statements from the article "A Horrible Way to Die," you can conclude that the authors want the reader to think that

☐ a. the Ebola virus is extremely powerful and dangerous.

☐ b. only Africans need to worry about dying of the Ebola virus.

☐ c. the Ebola virus might return and kill more victims.

4. What do the authors imply by saying "Doctors took blood samples from some of the victims. They rushed the samples to the United States. Doctors at the Centers for Disease Control (CDC) in Atlanta, Georgia, studied the samples"?

☐ a. The CDC is known around the world for studying and keeping track of diseases.

☐ b. There was no hospital in Africa that was able to study blood.

☐ c. Doctors in the United States were the only ones who were interested in studying the blood of the victims.

_____ Number of correct answers

Record your personal assessment of your work on the Critical Thinking Chart on page 150.

Summarizing and Paraphrasing

Put an X in the box next to the correct answer for questions 1 and 3. Follow the directions provided for question 2.

1. Below are summaries of the article. Choose the summary that says all the most important things about the article but in the fewest words.

☐ a. In 1995 the Ebola virus struck in Zaire, Africa, killing 315 people in a hideous way. Doctors believe the virus spreads through contact with the victim's blood. The virus may live in host animals in the rain forest and when humans enter the forest, the chances of picking up the virus increase.

☐ b. Thirty-six-year-old Kimfumu was among the first people to die of the Ebola virus in the 1995 outbreak in Africa. The nun who nursed him also died of the disease. The virus eventually killed 315 people before it died out.

☐ c. The Ebola virus kills its victims in a terrible way. The victim gets a headache and diarrhea. His or her organs turn to mush. Finally, the victim's nose, ears, and eyes begin to bleed. The disease may be passed from one person to another easily.

2. Reread paragraph 9 in the article. Below, write a summary of the paragraph in no more than 25 words.

_____

_____

_____

_____

Reread your summary and decide whether it covers the important ideas in the paragraph. Next, decide how to shorten the summary to 15 words or less without leaving out any essential information. Write this summary below.

_____

_____

_____

3. Choose the sentence that correctly restates the following sentence from the article "By the time outside doctors arrived, many patients and staff members had fled in fear."

☐ a. When doctors from other countries arrived, many patients and staff ran away from them.

☐ b. When outside doctors got there, they discovered that many patients and staff members had run away because they were so afraid.

☐ c. Outside doctors escaped, along with many patients and staff members, fearing the worst.

_____ Number of correct answers

Record your personal assessment of your work on the Critical Thinking Chart on page 150.

Critical Thinking

Put an X in the box next to the correct answer for questions 1, 2, and 4. Follow the directions provided for the other questions.

1. Which of the following statements from the article is an opinion rather than a fact?

   ☐ a. "It's useless for us to do anything."

   ☐ b. Ebola was first identified in 1976.

   ☐ c. By May 26, 121 people had died of Ebola.

2. From what the article said about the Ebola virus, you can predict that

   ☐ a. it will return someday and kill more humans.

   ☐ b. it will soon die out forever.

   ☐ c. in the future, the virus will not be dangerous to humans.

3. Choose from the letters below to correctly complete the following statement. Write the letters on the lines.

   On the positive side, _____, but on the negative side,

   _____.

   a. the government of Zaire asked people to stay in their homes

   b. the virus had killed hundreds of people during a few months

   c. the virus finally died out by August 24

4. If you were a doctor, how could you use the information in the article to treat your patients?

   ☐ a. Never touch the blood of Ebola victims.

   ☐ b. Keep Ebola victims close to other patients.

   ☐ c. Refuse to treat Ebola victims, because they are beyond help and other people would benefit more from your services.

5. In which paragraph did you find your information or details to answer question 2? _____

_____ Number of correct answers

Record your personal assessment of your work on the Critical Thinking Chart on page 150.

Personal Response

If I were the author, I would add _____

_____

_____

because _____

_____

Self-Assessment

Which concepts or ideas from the article were difficult to understand?

_____

_____

Which were easy?

_____

_____

A Strangler Among Us

No one paid much attention to the first murder. After all, Boston had about 50 killings every year. The death of 55-year-old Anna Slesers looked like another isolated tragedy. She was found, strangled, in her home on June 14, 1962. Police figured a robber had killed her.

2   Less than three weeks later, though, two more women were found dead in their homes. They, too, had been strangled. The crimes fit the same pattern as the Slesers case. When the

If the man in this photo came to your apartment door in plumbers' overalls, would you let him in? Such costumes got Albert DeSalvo into the homes of several of his victims. DeSalvo, known as the Boston Strangler, murdered 13 women before his arrest in 1964.

police commissioner heard that, he felt sick. He knew he was not dealing with isolated killings. "Oh, God," he said. "We've got a madman loose."

3   And so began the panic that was to grip Boston for the next 18 months. Everyone began talking about the "Boston Strangler." The commissioner put extra detectives on the case. He canceled all police vacations. He set up a special emergency number that people could call anytime, day or night.

4   Beyond that, police urged women to keep their doors locked. They told people not to let strangers into their homes. The police also asked citizens to report any suspicious activity they saw.

5   But it did no good. In August, the killer struck again. Two more women were strangled. They were 75-year-old Ida Irga and 67-year-old Jane Sullivan. Both were found dead in their apartments. Police were sure it was the work of the strangler. For one thing, there was no sign of forced entry. Both Irga and Sullivan—like the others—had let the killer in without a fight. As in the other cases, the apartments had been ransacked, but nothing had been taken. Finally, the murderer had left his

"signature": a bow, tied and knotted in a special way around the victims' necks.

6   Now the people of Boston were really petrified. Women refused to open their doors to delivery men. They screamed when salesmen rang their doorbells. Local hardware stores sold out of security locks. The Animal Rescue League couldn't keep up with the demand for watchdogs. Every day, women in tears called the police to report strange-looking men near their buildings.

7   One woman, who was expecting a visit from a friend, heard a knock on her door. She opened it. But instead of her friend, she was met by a man she had never seen before. Was it the Boston Strangler? Actually, it was someone selling encyclopedias. But the woman didn't know that. She was so terrified that she had a heart attack and dropped dead on the spot.

8   As panic swept through the city, the police struggled to find the killer. They looked at every possible clue. All the victims were white women over the age of 50. Did the killer meet them at some event for the elderly? All the dead women were also big music lovers. Did the strangler find them at concerts or

music stores? Or perhaps the answer lay in a different direction. All the victims were somehow connected to hospitals. They either worked at one or had just been treated at one. Was the killer also connected to hospitals in some way?

9   These possibilities led nowhere. And in the meantime, the killings continued. By the end of the year, the strangler had claimed two more victims. These two, however, were different. Both women were young—in their early 20s. In addition, one was black. The strangler was varying his crimes. With his next victim, he added another twist. This woman was found stabbed as well as strangled. Nonetheless, many details of the crime were the same. The murders all seemed to have been carried out by one man.

10   Police were frustrated. Everyone had been warned about the Boston Strangler, yet again and again he was able to talk his way into his victims' apartments. How was he doing it? And why?

11   One clue came from a woman named Gertrude Gruen. She lived through an attack by the Boston Strangler. In February of 1963, someone knocked on her apartment door. It was a man

dressed in workman's clothing. He told her he had come to fix a leak in her bathroom. There were other workmen in the area, so she assumed he was part of the same crew. She let him in. But when she turned her back on him, he threw his arm around her neck and tried to strangle her.

12 Gruen kicked and thrashed, trying to get away. She managed to grab her attacker's finger between her teeth. Then she bit down hard, almost to the bone. He loosened his hold on her for a minute and she screamed. Through the window, she could see workmen on the roof turn and look in her direction. The strangler must have seen them too. He released her and fled from the apartment.

13 Gruen's story didn't explain why the strangler killed women. But it did help explain how he got into their apartments. After that, real repairmen found it harder and harder to get their work done. Many women simply would not let them in. And some women didn't stop there. They began toting tear gas bombs in their purses. Some carried long hatpins with them wherever they went. They hoped to fend off any attack with one sharp jab of the pin. Some women even took up karate.

14 Nothing, however, seemed to stop the strangler. By January of 1964, the death toll stood at 13. The victims were all women, but beyond that, no clear pattern emerged. The victims ranged in age from 19 to 85. Some had been killed on weekends, some during the week. Most lived alone, but a couple had roommates. Most were white, but one was black. Most had been strangled with a pair of stockings, but one had been stabbed and one had been beaten to death with a brass pipe.

15 Police followed up on every lead they got, no matter how unlikely it seemed. They fed all the information they had into computers, hoping to find a link to some known criminal. They even turned to psychics for help.

16 In the end, though, it was the strangler himself who solved the case. In the fall of 1964, a man was arrested for breaking into a home. The intruder was 33-year-old Albert DeSalvo. He had been in trouble before. In fact, he had just been released from prison in April 1962. That was two months before the strangler first struck. Police had no idea that DeSalvo was connected to the killings. But he gave himself away. He bragged to a cellmate, saying he was the Boston Strangler.

17 When police heard this, they questioned DeSalvo about it. Yes, he said, he had committed the murders. He could not explain what had prompted him to kill. And he could not explain why he had chosen those particular women. Yet he knew dozens of details that only the killer could have known. And so in the end, there could be no doubt. DeSalvo was the Boston Strangler. When the people of Boston learned that the madman had been caught, they all breathed a sigh of relief. Now, after months of terror, the city could finally return to normal.

If you have been timed while reading this article, enter your reading time below. Then turn to the Words-per-Minute Table on page 147 and look up your reading speed (words per minute). Enter your reading speed on the graph on page 148.

Reading Time: Lesson 12

——————— : ———————
Minutes   *Seconds*

A Finding the Main Idea

One statement below expresses the main idea of the article. One statement is too general, or too broad. The other statement explains only part of the article; it is too narrow. Label the statements using the following key:

M—Main Idea   **B—Too Broad**   **N—Too Narrow**

_____ 1. At one time, all of the strangler's victims were white women over the age of 50.

_____ 2. For 18 months, women in the city of Boston were in a state of panic.

_____ 3. During a period in the 1960s, a madman who strangled women terrorized Boston.

_____ Score 15 points for a correct M answer.

_____ Score 5 points for each correct B or N answer.

_____ **Total Score:** Finding the Main Idea

B Recalling Facts

How well do you remember the facts in the article? Put an X in the box next to the answer that correctly completes each statement about the article.

1. One clue that one person did all the crimes was
   □ a. the same fingerprints at each scene.
   □ b. a special bow tied around the victims' necks.
   □ c. a special perfume left at each scene.

2. One woman had a heart attack when she saw
   □ a. one of the strangler's victims.
   □ b. the strangler.
   □ c. an encyclopedia salesman at her door.

3. Gretchen Gruen escaped the strangler by
   □ a. screaming and attracting attention.
   □ b. begging him to stop.
   □ c. running away.

4. Albert DeSalvo was arrested for
   □ a. robbing a convenience store.
   □ b. breaking into a home.
   □ c. attacking a woman on the street.

5. The way the strangler chose his victims was
   □ a. never fully explained.
   □ b. by meeting them at hospitals.
   □ c. by selecting them at concerts.

Score 5 points for each correct answer.

_____ **Total Score:** Recalling Facts

C | Making Inferences

When you combine your own experience with information from a text to draw a conclusion that is not directly stated in that text, you are making an inference. Below are five statements that may or may not be inferences based on information in the article. Label the statements using the following key:

C—Correct Inference   F—Faulty Inference

_____ 1. Boston has more killings per year than any other major American city.

_____ 2. Someone in jail with Albert DeSalvo helped the police crack the case.

_____ 3. The strangler must have looked harmless to the women who let him into their homes.

_____ 4. A good summer job in 1963 would have been selling items door-to-door in Boston.

_____ 5. Any murders committed in Boston after the fall of 1964 were the work of someone other than the Boston Strangler.

Score 5 points for each correct answer.

_____ **Total Score:** Making Inferences

D | Using Words Precisely

Each numbered sentence below contains an underlined word or phrase from the article. Following the sentence are three definitions. One definition is closest to the meaning of the underlined word. One definition is opposite or nearly opposite. Label those two definitions using the following key; do not label the remaining definition.

C—Closest   O—Opposite or Nearly Opposite

1. The death of 55-year-old Anna Slesers looked like another <u>isolated</u> tragedy.

☐ a. common

☐ b. unconnected

☐ c. sad

2. As in the other cases, the apartments had been <u>ransacked</u>, but nothing had been taken.

☐ a. set afire

☐ b. neatly arranged

☐ c. searched wildly or carelessly

3. Now the people of Boston were really <u>petrified</u>.

☐ a. reassured

☐ b. curious

☐ c. frightened

4. They began <u>toting</u> tear gas bombs in their purses.

☐ a. carrying

☐ b. removing

☐ c. discharging

5. And he could not explain why he had chosen those <u>particular</u> women.

☐ a. middle-aged

☐ b. specific; individual

☐ c. general groups of

___

Enter the four total scores in the spaces below, and add them together to find your Reading Comprehension Score. Then record your score on the graph on page 149.

Author's Approach

Put an X in the box next to the correct answer.

1. What is the authors' purpose in writing "A Strangler Among Us"?

☐ a. to encourage readers to lock their doors

☐ b. to inform readers about the death of Anna Slesers

☐ c. to describe a situation in which a city was terrorized by one criminal

2. Which of the following statements from the article best describes the most compelling reason why police believed that Albert DeSalvo was the Boston Strangler?

☐ a. [Albert DeSalvo] had been in trouble before.

☐ b. Yet he knew dozens of details that only the killer could have known.

☐ c. He bragged to a cellmate, saying he was the Boston Strangler.

3. In this article, ". . . the murderer had left his 'signature': a bow, tied and knotted in a special way around the victims' necks" means that the killer

☐ a. had left behind a unique clue that identified the crime as his.

☐ b. had left behind a clue that was common to almost all murder cases.

☐ c. signed his name to a bow tied around the victims' necks.

4. The authors tell this story mainly by

☐ a. telling about events in the order they happened.

☐ b. comparing different topics.

☐ c. using his or her imagination and creativity.

___

_____ Number of correct answers

Record your personal assessment of your work on the Critical Thinking Chart on page 150.

Summarizing and Paraphrasing

Follow the directions provided for question 1. Put an X in the box next to the correct answer for question 2.

1. Look for the important ideas and events in paragraphs 1 and 2. Summarize those paragraphs in one or two sentences.

_____

_____

_____

_____

2. Read the statement from the article below. Then read the paraphrase of that statement. Choose the reason that best tells why the paraphrase does not say the same thing as the statement.

    Statement: Police urged women not to let strangers into their homes, no matter how innocent they seemed to be.

    Paraphrase: Although police urged women not to admit strangers to their homes, the strangler's victims were letting him in.

    ☐ a. Paraphrase says too much.

    ☐ b. Paraphrase doesn't say enough.

    ☐ c. Paraphrase doesn't agree with the statement.

_____ Number of correct answers

Record your personal assessment of your work on the Critical Thinking Chart on page 150.

Critical Thinking

Follow the directions provided for questions 1, 3, and 5. Put an X in the box next to the correct answer for the other questions.

1. For each statement below, write *O* if it expresses an opinion or write *F* if it expresses a fact.

    _____ a. If the police had worked harder on the case, they could have solved it sooner.

    _____ b. One woman died of a heart attack after opening her door to a stranger selling encyclopedias.

    _____ c. Some women went overboard in arming themselves against the strangler.

2. Considering what happened to Gertrude Gruen as told in this article, you can predict that she will

    ☐ a. suspect every stranger at her door of being the Boston Strangler.

    ☐ b. feel perfectly safe now that the Boston Strangler has been arrested.

    ☐ c. ask any workers who come to her door for proper identification.

3. Think about cause-effect relationships in the article. Fill in the blanks in the cause-effect chart, drawing from the letters below.

Cause	Effect
Gertrude Gruen screamed loudly.	_____
Gertrude Gruen bit down hard on her attacker's finger.	_____
The man ringing Gertrude Gruen's doorbell said he had come to fix a leak.	_____

 a. Gertrude Gruen let her attacker into her apartment.

 b. Workmen looked in her direction.

 c. The man loosened his grip on her.

4. How is the story of the Boston Strangler related to the theme of *Total Panic*?

 ☐ a. The Boston Strangler ransacked the apartments of his victims' before killing them.

 ☐ b. Fear of the strangler made the women of Boston frantic for months.

 ☐ c. Police finally caught up with the killer and arrested him.

5. Which paragraphs from the article provide evidence that supports

 your answer to question 3? _____

_____ Number of correct answers

Record your personal assessment of your work on the Critical Thinking Chart on page 150.

Personal Response

What new question do you have about this topic?

_____

_____

_____

_____

Self-Assessment

While reading the article, I found it easiest to _____

_____

_____

_____

_____

The Richard Riot

Angry fans attack Clarence Campbell, the president of the National Hockey League, during a game at the Forum in Montreal, Canada. The violence quickly spread to the city's streets.

Canadians knew there might be trouble. Still, on the night of March 17, 1955, ice hockey fans turned out in force. They packed the Forum in the Quebec city of Montreal. They were not in a happy mood. To make things worse, the most-hated man in Quebec had announced that he would be at the game. It seemed only a matter of time. Sooner or later, a riot was sure to break out.

2   That most-hated man was Clarence Campbell, president of the National Hockey League. He had just suspended Maurice "The Rocket" Richard (Ree `shard) for the rest of the year. A week earlier, Richard had twice swung his hockey stick at another player. Such violent acts sometimes happen in hockey. Most of the time the players involved get a fine or a short suspension. But this time Campbell had cracked down really hard.

3   If it had happened to a lesser player, the fans' anger might just have blown over. But Richard was a superstar. He was the best player on the Montreal Canadiens. Without him, the team had little chance of winning the Stanley Cup.

4   And there was more. Richard was a symbol of great pride for the people of Quebec. Like most people from Quebec, Richard spoke French. That set him apart from people in other parts of Canada. Campbell was from an English-speaking part of Canada. So to some fans, it seemed as if Campbell was punishing not just a player or a team but every French speaker in Quebec.

5   Newspapers and radio stations stirred up hatred for Campbell. A cartoon showed Campbell's head on a platter. The caption read: "This is how we would like to see him." One poll showed that 97 percent of the Quebec people surveyed felt the punishment was too harsh. Brian McKenna, who later made a film about Richard, was nine years old at the time. He said, "It was my first sense that maybe the world was unfair." Even the mayor of Montreal criticized Campbell's decision.

6   To add more heat to the simmering pot, Campbell announced that he would be at the Forum on March 17. The mayor begged him to stay home. But Campbell wanted to go. He often went to games there. He didn't see any reason why he should back down. "I have a right to go," he said.

7   Campbell was not there when the game began. A few minutes into the first period, Richard arrived with his wife. No one even noticed him. All eyes were on Campbell's empty seat. Halfway through the first period, the Detroit Red Wings took a 2–0 lead. Any hopes of the Canadiens' winning seemed to be evaporating. At that moment Campbell walked into the Forum. He didn't try to sneak in or come in disguise. He wanted the fans to know he wasn't afraid.

8   The crowd roared with disgust. They began to shout "Shoo Campbell, Shoo Campbell." A few fans threw eggs, tomatoes, and programs at him. At one point, a flying object knocked the hat off his head. An orange hit Campbell in the back. "This is a disgrace," muttered Richard, who saw what was happening.

9 Campbell refused to budge. During the intermission after the first period, a fan walked up to Campbell's aisle seat. The man stuck out his hand as if to offer a handshake. Campbell put out his hand. But instead of shaking Campbell's hand, the fan slapped his face. Many outraged fans rushed to surround Campbell. Would they kill him?

10 We will never know. At that moment, someone in the crowd tossed a tear-gas bomb only 25 feet from Campbell. Everyone panicked. They forgot about Campbell. All they wanted was to get out of the Forum as fast as possible. "The bomb-thrower," said a police chief, "protected Campbell's life by releasing [the bomb] at precisely the right moment."

11 Campbell fled to the first-aid center. "This is terrible," he said. "People might have been killed." He then called off the rest of the game and declared it a forfeit in favor of the Red Wings.

12 By then, frightened fans had rushed out onto the street. Once there, some of them vented their rage. They began what would be called "The Richard Riot." It was started by only a few hundred troublemakers. But, as in any mob scene, others got swept up in the madness. In a short time, a mob of more than 10,000 people was shouting "Kill Campbell!" Gangs of mostly young fans broke windows, set fires, tipped over cars, and looted stores. This continued for four long hours. By the time the riot petered out, police had arrested 137 people.

13 Earlier, Richard had left the Forum by a back door. At home, he listened to riot reports on the radio. He couldn't believe what was being done in his name. He felt badly. "Once I felt like going downtown and telling the people over a loudspeaker to stop their nonsense," Richard said. "But it wouldn't have done any good. They would have carried me around on their shoulders." Richard thought it was nice to have fans support him, but he knew these fans were doing it the wrong way.

14 Fortunately, no one was killed. Still, many people in Montreal felt remorse. The next day one sportswriter wrote, "I am ashamed of my city."

15 Others, however, still blamed Campbell. They said he had provoked the riot by showing up. Some still mumbled about getting even. The threat of a second riot hung in the air. Hoping to diffuse the dangerous situation, Richard decided to speak up.

16 On March 18 he spoke in French to his fans. He said it was hard not being able to play, but there was nothing he could do about it. He urged his fans to stop all the violence. "So that no further harm will be done," he added, "I would like to ask everyone to get behind the team and to help the boys win. . . . I will take my punishment and come back next year to help the club."

17 Richard's speech calmed the city. There was no more violence. But in the long run, the Richard Riot helped spark a new movement in Canada that is still alive today. It had nothing to do with hockey. It had to do with the French people of Quebec. They began a long fight to preserve their culture and language. Some even wanted to make Quebec a separate nation.

18 This movement has been called the Quiet Revolution. Sportswriter Red Fisher was covering his first game ever on the night of the Richard Riot. Fisher later wrote, "If that was the start of the Quiet Revolution, it wasn't very quiet."

If you have been timed while reading this article, enter your reading time below. Then turn to the Words-per-Minute Table on page 147 and look up your reading speed (words per minute). Enter your reading speed on the graph on page 148.

Reading Time: Lesson 13

_____ : _____
Minutes   Seconds

A | Finding the Main Idea

One statement below expresses the main idea of the article. One statement is too general, or too broad. The other statement explains only part of the article; it is too narrow. Label the statements using the following key:

M—Main Idea   **B—Too Broad**   **N—Too Narrow**

_____ 1. In 1955 in Montreal, Canada, when a French-speaking hockey player was suspended by the English-speaking league president, angry fans rioted.

_____ 2. Hockey superstar Maurice Richard was suspended for the rest of the year after swinging his hockey stick twice at another player.

_____ 3. Fans' emotions run high during important games, especially when the fans believe an injustice has been done.

_____ Score 15 points for a correct M answer.

_____ Score 5 points for each correct B or N answer.

_____ **Total Score:** Finding the Main Idea

B | Recalling Facts

How well do you remember the facts in the article? Put an X in the box next to the answer that correctly completes each statement about the article.

1. Clarence Campbell was
   ☐ a. the president of the National Hockey League.
   ☐ b. the best ice hockey player on the Montreal Canadiens team.
   ☐ c. the mayor of Montreal.

2. Maurice Richard spoke
   ☐ a. English.
   ☐ b. Spanish.
   ☐ c. French.

3. One fan who seemed ready to shake Campbell's hand
   ☐ a. knocked Campbell's hat off his head instead.
   ☐ b. threw an orange at Campbell instead.
   ☐ c. slapped Campbell in the face instead.

4. By the end of the riot, police had arrested
   ☐ a. 137 people.
   ☐ b. 2,000 people.
   ☐ c. 10,000 people.

5. After the riot Maurice Richard felt
   ☐ a. proud of the rioting fans.
   ☐ b. ashamed of the rioting fans.
   ☐ c. angry with Clarence Campbell.

Score 5 points for each correct answer.

_____ **Total Score:** Recalling Facts

C Making Inferences

When you combine your own experience with information from a text to draw a conclusion that is not directly stated in that text, you are making an inference. Below are five statements that may or may not be inferences based on information in the article. Label the statements using the following key:

C—Correct Inference   **F—Faulty Inference**

_____ 1. Clarence Campbell did not expect that his presence at the game would start a violent riot.

_____ 2. There were no police or security forces at the Forum on the night of the riot.

_____ 3. Many people were badly injured during the riot.

_____ 4. Montreal shopkeepers were angry with the rioters.

_____ 5. If the Richard Riot hadn't occurred, there would have been no Quiet Revolution.

Score 5 points for each correct answer.

_____ **Total Score:** Making Inferences

D Using Words Precisely

Each numbered sentence below contains an underlined word or phrase from the article. Following the sentence are three definitions. One definition is closest to the meaning of the underlined word. One definition is opposite or nearly opposite. Label those two definitions using the following key; do not label the remaining definition.

C—Closest   **O—Opposite or Nearly Opposite**

1. Most of the time the players involved get a <u>fine</u> or a short suspension.

_____ a. reward

_____ b. money penalty

_____ c. news article

2. Any hopes of the Canadiens' winning seemed to be <u>evaporating</u>.

_____ a. frightening

_____ b. growing

_____ c. disappearing

3. The crowd roared with <u>disgust</u>.

_____ a. anger and hatred

_____ b. surprise

_____ c. delight

4. "This is a <u>disgrace</u>," muttered Richard, who saw what was happening.

_____ a. game

_____ b. dishonor

_____ c. proud moment

5. By the time the riot <u>petered out</u>, police had arrested 137 people.

_____ a. died away

_____ b. strengthened

_____ c. moved

_____ Score 3 points for each correct C answer.

_____ Score 2 points for each correct O answer.

_____ **Total Score:** Using Words Precisely

Enter the four total scores in the spaces below, and add them together to find your Reading Comprehension Score. Then record your score on the graph on page 149.

Score	Question Type	Lesson 13
_____	Finding the Main Idea	
_____	Recalling Facts	
_____	Making Inferences	
_____	Using Words Precisely	
_____	**Reading Comprehension Score**	

Author's Approach

Put an X in the box next to the correct answer.

1. The main purpose of the first paragraph is to

☐ a. explain why Richard was suspended.

☐ b. express an opinion about Richard's suspension.

☐ c. describe the setting of the riot.

2. From the statements below, choose those that you believe the author would agree with.

☐ a. If Campbell hadn't attended the game, there probably would have been no riot there.

☐ b. Richard was to blame for the riot.

☐ c. Richard acted like a gentleman during and after the game.

3. Choose the statement below that is the weakest argument for rioting.

☐ a. Rioting sometimes leads to positive change.

☐ b. Rioting can lead to destruction of property, injuries, and even death.

☐ c. Rioting can send a message to authorities to show that people are unhappy.

4. The author probably wrote this article to

☐ a. tell about a situation in which people were out of control.

☐ b. explain the thinking behind the Quiet Revolution.

☐ c. support the preservation of French language and customs in Quebec.

_____ Number of correct answers

Record your personal assessment of your work on the Critical Thinking Chart on page 150.

Summarizing and Paraphrasing

Follow the directions provided for questions 1 and 2. Put an X in the box next to the correct answer for question 3.

1. Complete the following one-sentence summary of the article using the lettered phrases from the phrase bank below. Write the letters on the lines.

> **Phrase Bank**
>
> a. Richard's reaction to the riot and an explanation of the effects of the riot
> b. how the riot began at the hockey game
> c. an explanation of why Canadiens fans were upset

The article "The Richard Riot" begins with _____, goes on

to explain _____, and ends with _____.

2. Reread paragraph 6 in the article. Below, write a summary of the paragraph in no more than 25 words.

_____

_____

_____

_____

Reread your summary and decide whether it covers the important ideas in the paragraph. Next, decide how to shorten the summary to 15 words or less without leaving out any essential information. Write this summary below.

_____

_____

_____

3. Choose the best one-sentence paraphrase for the following sentence from the article "[Campbell] then called off the rest of the game and declared it a forfeit in favor of the Red Wings."

☐ a. Campbell acted as the referee for the rest of the game and called all the plays in favor of the Red Wings.

☐ b. Campbell didn't allow the game to continue, and he proclaimed that the Red Wings had forfeited the game.

☐ c. Campbell stopped the game and declared that the Canadiens had forfeited the game to the Red Wings.

> _____ Number of correct answers
>
> Record your personal assessment of your work on the Critical Thinking Chart on page 150.

Critical Thinking

Put an X in the box next to the correct answer for questions 1, 3, 4, and 5. Follow the directions provided for question 2.

1. Which of the following statements from the article is an opinion rather than a fact?

☐ a. Halfway through the first period, the Detroit Red Wings took a 2–0 lead.

☐ b. If it had happened to a lesser player, the fans' anger might just have blown over.

☐ c. Gangs of mostly young fans broke windows, set fires, tipped over cars, and looted stores.

2. Using what you know about Clarence Campbell and what is told about Maurice Richard in the article, name three ways Campbell is similar to and three ways Campbell is different from Richard. Cite the paragraph number(s) where you found details in the article to support your conclusions.

Similarities

_____

_____

_____

Differences

_____

_____

_____

3. What was the effect of Richard's plea for peace?

☐ a. The rioting stopped.

☐ b. The rioting increased.

☐ c. Campbell was forced to resign.

4. Of the following theme categories, which one would this story fit into?

☐ a. Don't let your enemies stop you from doing whatever you want to do.

☐ b. Sometimes it is wiser not to provoke your enemies.

☐ c. People in crowds always act responsibly.

5. What did you have to do to answer question 2?

☐ a. find a comparison (how things are the same)

☐ b. find a summary (general idea)

☐ c. find a cause (why something happened)

_____ Number of correct answers

Record your personal assessment of your work on the Critical Thinking Chart on page 150.

Personal Response

I know how Clarence Campbell felt because _____

_____

_____

_____

Self-Assessment

While reading the article, I found it easiest to _____

_____

_____

_____

A Volcano Wakes Up

Sure, El Chichón was a volcano. But it had not erupted in many, many years. In fact, most scientists said the volcano had been inactive for thousands of years. El Chichón was also quite small—it was really little more than a hill. It stood only 4,134 feet high. Even its name wasn't scary. In the local language, *chichón* means "lump."

2   So there was no need to worry. Or was there? A volcano will often give some warning signs before it erupts.

A column of volcanic smoke and ash from El Chichón rises 12,000 feet above the village of El Volcan. Residents of the town, like everyone else living in this area of southern Mexico, were driven away when the small mountain suddenly erupted on March 28, 1982.

El Chichón, in southern Mexico, began sending out such signals in the early 1980s. For months the earth made rumbling sounds. There were even a few small earthquakes. A cloud of steam appeared over El Chichón. Also, the water in local rivers began heating up and giving off the odor of sulfur.

3 These were all hints that the volcano might erupt. But they offered no guarantee. Maybe nothing would happen. Officials said the earth in the region had always rumbled. They declared that the cloud of steam had always been there. So nothing was done. The Zoque Indians who lived near El Chichón were never instructed to move out. That turned out to be a terrible mistake.

4 By March of 1982, the rumblings had grown stronger. At last, scientists decided to check things out. But they didn't act quickly enough. Late on the night of March 28, El Chichón blew its top. It spewed ash 10 miles into the darkening sky.

5 As the ash fell back to earth, it covered everything. "About a billion tons of ash fell over a 10-square-mile area," said one official. The volcano also shot out hot gases and rocks. "There's nothing left on the mountain," said one man, "only stones and ashes."

6 Those who lived nearby had little or no chance to get away. The volcano rained down fire and ash on local villages. It totally wiped out several communities. One of these was called Nicalpa. It was located just four miles from the volcano. "My five children burned to death," said one resident. "When I went to look for them, I found only ashes. The house wasn't there anymore."

7 Another man was away from Nicalpa at the time. But when he returned, he found his farm destroyed. "I had 20 cattle and a few horses," he said sadly. "The fire that came burned everything. I had corn, beans, and coffee, and everything now is flat ground." Some of his friends were not even that lucky. One family of seven was caught near the village. The entire family died.

8 The March 28 eruption was bad enough, but the worst was yet to come. A volcano is difficult to predict. Will it produce just one eruption or will there be others? If there is more than one, how big will the next ones be? Not even the experts could answer those questions. The people who lived just out of range of the first explosion didn't know what to do. Should they stay in their homes? Should they leave? In the end, officials decided these people had to be evacuated. Many were forced out of their homes against their will. Some refused to stay away and quickly snuck back to their villages.

9 Tragically for them, on April 2, El Chichón acted up again. It began sending out more ash and gas. The noon sky turned black. Many people were really frightened, fearing the darkening sky was a sign from God. They believed that they were being punished for their sins. Most of these people felt certain that they were all about to die. A local priest spoke to them over the radio, trying to calm their fears. The priest explained that the darkness was caused by the ash in the air. It was just a natural phenomenon.

10 Most villagers listened to the priest. But the following day, El Chichón erupted again. This was the worst explosion of all. Gas, ash, and rocks came pouring out of the volcano. One man said, "It looked like fireworks

were blasting out of the [volcano's] top." The eruption continued into the next day. Thousands of people fled their homes. Some made it to safety; many didn't.

11   This time, the volcano reached as far as the town of Pichucalco, about 15 miles away. Ash and rocks caused tremendous damage there. The roof of the new market collapsed, as did the roof of the town's only movie theater. "The fire started coming out of the sky," said one man. "[The] rocks came through the roof like bullets." These "fire rocks," as they were called, burned and injured many people.

12   The blast wiped out the small village of Francisco León. It was located in a valley, so the flow of burning lava was funneled straight into it. The lava turned the village's fertile fields into a barren desert. It turned the trees into charcoal. And it turned people's dreams to dust.

13   Everyone who was caught in the village died. Rescue workers didn't reach the area until two weeks later.

They found the whole place buried under ash. Only a small section of the church wall was still visible. The first body they dug up was that of a little boy. He was hugging his small dog.

14   El Chichón was a major eruption. After the blast, the top 700 feet of the mountain were gone. The blast sent a huge amount of ash into the air. This ash affected the world's weather. High in the atmosphere, the ash reflected sunlight away from the planet. That, in turn, lowered temperatures on Earth.

15   For the Zoque Indians, the effect was direct and devastating. The volcano destroyed their homes and villages. It wiped out their farms. And it killed entire families. The exact number of dead will never be known. The whole thing happened in a remote part of Mexico. Birth records were not always up-to-date. And, in any case, the ash and rocks buried people whose bodies will never be found.

16   The official count was 187 dead. But no one believes that. The real figure is

likely in the thousands. The *World Almanac* puts the number of dead at 1,880. Whatever the number, this was a major disaster for the people of the region.

17   Now, of course, scientists are taking El Chichón more seriously. These days, it is considered to be a young, active volcano. Experts believe that it will erupt again. And this time it may not take thousands of years to do so.

If you have been timed while reading this article, enter your reading time below. Then turn to the Words-per-Minute Table on page 147 and look up your reading speed (words per minute). Enter your reading speed on the graph on page 148.

Reading Time: Lesson 14

———— : ————
Minutes   Seconds

A | Finding the Main Idea

One statement below expresses the main idea of the article. One statement is too general, or too broad. The other statement explains only part of the article; it is too narrow. Label the statements using the following key:

M—Main Idea   B—Too Broad   N—Too Narrow

_____ 1. Although volcanoes are often inactive for long periods of time, they may still be dangerous.

_____ 2. The eruption of El Chichón in a remote area of Mexico caused widespread death and damage.

_____ 3. The eruption of El Chichón caused a rain of about a billion tons of ash over a 10-square-mile area.

_____ Score 15 points for a correct M answer.

_____ Score 5 points for each correct B or N answer.

_____ **Total Score:** Finding the Main Idea

B | Recalling Facts

How well do you remember the facts in the article? Put an X in the box next to the answer that correctly completes each statement about the article.

1. El Chichón began sending out hints that it might erupt during the early
   ☐ a. 1960s.
   ☐ b. 1970s.
   ☐ c. 1980s.

2. Scientists believed the volcano had last erupted
   ☐ a. thousands of years ago.
   ☐ b. about 200 years ago.
   ☐ c. about 90 years ago.

3. El Chichón's most dangerous eruptions took place
   ☐ a. January 3 and 4, 1982.
   ☐ b. April 2 and 3, 1982.
   ☐ c. October 3 and 4, 1982.

4. Daytime skies became dark because
   ☐ a. the people had been evil.
   ☐ b. an eclipse occurred at the same time.
   ☐ c. a great deal of ash filled the air.

5. The exact death toll will never be known because
   ☐ a. birth records in that part of Mexico were not up-to-date.
   ☐ b. search teams are not allowed in the area.
   ☐ c. no one cares.

Score 5 points for each correct answer.

_____ **Total Score:** Recalling Facts

C | Making Inferences

When you combine your own experience with information from a text to draw a conclusion that is not directly stated in that text, you are making an inference. Below are five statements that may or may not be inferences based on information in the article. Label the statements using the following key:

C—Correct Inference   **F—Faulty Inference**

_____ 1. During the volcano's eruption, people in wooden houses would have been safer than those in brick homes.

_____ 2. The eruptions would have been especially dangerous to people with breathing problems.

_____ 3. El Chichón probably would have been studied more carefully if it had been near a major city.

_____ 4. Modern science has found ways to predict such natural events with certainty.

_____ 5. Your weather can be affected by events that take place far away from you.

Score 5 points for each correct answer.

_____ **Total Score:** Making Inferences

D | Using Words Precisely

Each numbered sentence below contains an underlined word or phrase from the article. Following the sentence are three definitions. One definition is closest to the meaning of the underlined word. One definition is opposite or nearly opposite. Label those two definitions using the following key; do not label the remaining definition.

C—Closest   **O—Opposite or Nearly Opposite**

1. A volcano will often give some warning signs before it erupts.
☐ a. remains inactive
☐ b. freezes
☐ c. bursts out with force

2. But they offered no guarantee.
☐ a. uncertainty
☐ b. promise with certainty
☐ c. signal

3. It spewed ash 10 miles into the sky.
☐ a. spit out
☐ b. spotted
☐ c. drew in

4. In the end, officials decided these people had to be evacuated.
☐ a. moved out
☐ b. sent in
☐ c. heard

5. The lava turned the village's fertile fields into a <u>barren</u> desert.

☐ a. mountainous

☐ b. fruitful; rich with life

☐ c. unable to support life or growth

_____ Score 3 points for each correct C answer.

_____ Score 2 points for each correct O answer.

_____ **Total Score:** Using Words Precisely

Enter the four total scores in the spaces below, and add them together to find your Reading Comprehension Score. Then record your score on the graph on page 149.

Score	Question Type	Lesson 14
_____	Finding the Main Idea	
_____	Recalling Facts	
_____	Making Inferences	
_____	Using Words Precisely	
_____	**Reading Comprehension Score**	

Author's Approach

Put an X in the box next to the correct answer.

1. Which of the following statements from the article best describes the effects of the volcano eruption?

☐ a. In fact, most scientists said the volcano had been inactive for thousands of years.

☐ b. The volcano rained down fire and ash on local villages.

☐ c. The whole thing happened in a remote part of Mexico.

2. Judging by statements from the article "A Volcano Wakes Up," you can conclude that the authors want the reader to think that

☐ a. the eruption caused a great deal of suffering and damage.

☐ b. this eruption was not particularly serious.

☐ c. the people around the volcano fully understood the risk they were taking by staying near it.

3. Choose the statement below that best describes the authors' position in paragraph 4.

☐ a. Scientists had no reason to check out the volcano until March 1982.

☐ b. El Chichón's eruption was entirely unexpected.

☐ c. Scientists should have checked out the volcano earlier.

4. The authors probably wrote this article to

☐ a. discourage people from living near volcanoes.

☐ b. teach the reader why volcanoes erupt.

☐ c. inform the reader of a destructive volcano that caused panic.

_____ Number of correct answers

Record your personal assessment of your work on the Critical Thinking Chart on page 150.

Summarizing and Paraphrasing

Follow the directions provided for questions 1 and 2. Put an X in the box next to the correct answer for question 3.

1. Complete the following one-sentence summary of the article using the lettered phrases from the phrase bank below. Write the letters on the lines.

    > **Phrase Bank**
    > a. the warning signs that the volcano was about to erupt
    > b. a summary of the damage the volcano did
    > c. what happened when the volcano erupted

    The article "A Volcano Wakes Up" begins with _____, goes

    on to explain _____, and ends with _____.

2. Reread paragraph 11 in the article. Below, write a summary of the paragraph in no more than 25 words.

    _____

    _____

    _____

    _____

    Reread your summary and decide whether it covers the important ideas in the paragraph. Next, decide how to shorten the summary to 15 words or less without leaving out any essential information. Write this summary below.

    _____

    _____

    _____

3. Choose the best one-sentence paraphrase for the following sentence from the article "High in the atmosphere, the ash reflected sunlight away from the planet."

    ☐ a. Sunlight from the planet was reflected by the ashes in the atmosphere.

    ☐ b. Ash reflected the sunlight into the planet's atmosphere.

    ☐ c. Ash high in the atmosphere reflected sunlight back into space.

    > _____ Number of correct answers
    >
    > Record your personal assessment of your work on the Critical Thinking Chart on page 150.

Critical Thinking

Follow the directions provided for the following questions.

1. For each statement below, write *O* if it expresses an opinion or write *F* if it expresses a fact.

    _____ a. Any experienced volcano watcher would have known when the volcano would erupt.

    _____ b. The local priest should not have tried to calm their fears.

    _____ c. The volcano erupted the first time on March 28, 1982.

CRITICAL THINKING

2. Choose from the letters below to correctly complete the following statement. Write the letters on the lines.

On the positive side, _____, but on the negative side,

_____.

   a.   El Chicón is a volcano

   b.   El Chicón finally stopped erupting

   c.   El Chicón may erupt again soon

3. Choose from the letters below to correctly complete the following statement. Write the letters on the lines.

According to the article, _____ caused sunlight to _____,

and the effect was that _____.

   a.   reflect away from the earth

   b.   temperatures on Earth were lowered

   c.   ash high in the atmosphere

4. In which paragraph did you find your information or details to

answer question 3? _____

_____ Number of correct answers

Record your personal assessment of your work on the Critical Thinking Chart on page 150.

Personal Response

What was most surprising or interesting to you about this article?

_____

_____

_____

_____

_____

Self-Assessment

Before reading this article, I already knew _____

_____

_____

_____

Death Rides the Subway

On March 20, 1995, a mysterious gas spread through the Tokyo subway system. Only the luckiest riders were able to stagger out. Twelve subway patrons died, and 5,500 more needed medical attention. Even during the cleanup, workers had to wear gas masks. Who was to blame for this disaster?

Six million people took the Tokyo subway each day. It was an easy, comfortable ride. People could grab a nap on the way to work or school.

The subway was clean—so clean that the workers who ran it wore white gloves. And it was safe. There were no gangs roaming the cars looking for trouble. Quiet, clean, and safe—the Tokyo subway stood as a symbol of modern Japan.

2   That image vanished on March 20, 1995. During the morning rush hour, terrorists struck. They planted a nerve gas called sarin on the subway. Sarin is extremely lethal in both its liquid and vapor forms. Less than one drop can easily kill a human. Sarin was invented in Germany in the 1930s. The Nazis used it in their death camps. Sarin attacks the lungs, causing people to suffocate. In minutes, its victims are dead.

3   That was what Tokyo's commuters were up against. Death was riding the subway that morning. But no one knew it. Probably only a handful of people had even heard of sarin. There was no reason to think it would ever show up in a subway.

4   The terrorists used lunch boxes and soft drink bottles to sneak the sarin into the subway. They left these items in trains on three different lines. The gas leaked out just as the three trains converged on the central station. Tokyo's police headquarters was just outside the station. Officials later said the terrorists had two goals. One was to kill as many people as possible. The other was to thumb their noses at the police.

5   Kasumasa Takahashi worked on the subway. His post was at the central station. A little after eight o'clock, a train pulled in. Takahashi noticed something strange. People began spilling out of the first car in pain. Some had tears rolling down their cheeks. Others were foaming at the mouth. "What's wrong?" cried Takahashi.

6   He ran over to the car. There he saw a small package wrapped in newspaper. Takahashi picked it up and carried it away. As he went, drops of liquid fell on the platform tiles. It looked like nothing more than water. So he stopped to wipe them up. As he bent over, he blacked out and collapsed. Takahashi died later that day in the hospital.

7   One woman was on her way to work. She got off a train at the central station. As she did so, she noticed a weird smell. "The smell was something I had never experienced," she said. She put a handkerchief over her mouth and began climbing the stairs to get out of the subway. Her head started to pound. Her vision became blurry. With each step she grew sicker and sicker. She had to fight back the urge to throw up. "When I got outside, I crouched down," she recalled. "So many people were like me, crouched on the ground."

8   This woman was one of thousands injured in the attack. They all stumbled out or were carried out of the subway gasping for fresh air. Many were bleeding from the nose and vomiting.

9   One victim didn't feel bad at first. But as he headed for his office, he began to

feel funny. "The sunlight suddenly seemed to brighten. My vision got hazy," he said. "I felt my chest being pressed, and my neck became stiff. I had a headache."

10   Twelve people died from their exposure to sarin that morning. More than 5,500 others were injured. The terrorists had shattered the city's sense of safety. They had planted fear in the hearts of the Japanese people. In the days that followed the attack, many of them refused to ride the subway. It was no longer a safe place to be.

11   Newspapers around the world condemned the attack. One Japanese paper called it "mass murder" and "an unthinkable crime." A U.S. paper described it as "ghastly." An Israeli paper called the terrorists "mindless criminals."

12   Who were these terrorists? In most cases, the guilty parties come forward to accept the blame. That's why they commit their crimes in the first place. Terrorists want people to pay attention to them. But this time no one stepped forward.

13   Still, the police had a pretty good idea who was behind the attack. They suspected it was a man named Shoko Asahara. He was the head of a religious sect known as the "Supreme Truth." Asahara was arrested. In his house,

the police found materials needed to make sarin. They also found millions of dollars in cash and gold. The police then charged Asahara with master-minding the attack.

14   Why would Asahara commit such an awful crime? It isn't clear. But he had certainly developed a twisted view of himself and of the world. For example, Asahara seemed to believe he could fly. He didn't need a plane, he said. He could do it all by himself. At one point, he claimed that he could stay aloft for three seconds. Even better days lay ahead. "Within a year," he predicted, "my body should be able to fly at will."

15   That wasn't his only strange boast. Asahara said that he could read people's minds. He claimed he could see into the future. And, like Superman, he said he had X-ray vision. All these skills he promised to teach his followers. Surprisingly, many people believed him. Asahara had 10,000 followers in Japan. He had 20,000 more in the rest of the world. These people were true believers. They turned over all their money to him. And each time they met him, they kissed his big toe.

16   Such nonsense was pretty harmless. But there was a much darker side to Asahara. He declared that the last world war would begin in 1997. The primary

weapon, he predicted, would be sarin. He told his followers to get ready for the coming battle. He told them they should welcome death.

17   One expert on terrorism explained that it is tough to deal with lunatics like Asahara. How do you fight someone, he asked "whose idea of a happy death is mass suicide?"

18   There was no easy answer for that. Toyko's commuters did slowly return to the subway. But fear continued to hang in the air. People now realized that terrorists could strike anywhere, even on a "safe" subway train in Japan.

A | Finding the Main Idea

One statement below expresses the main idea of the article. One statement is too general, or too broad. The other statement explains only part of the article; it is too narrow. Label the statements using the following key:

M—Main Idea   **B—Too Broad**   **N—Too Narrow**

_____ 1. In March 1995, terrorists used a poison called sarin to injure and kill commuters on a Tokyo subway.

_____ 2. Sarin, the poison chosen for the subway attack, was developed in Germany in the 1930s and used by the Nazis in their death camps.

_____ 3. The subways of Tokyo can no longer be considered to be safe because of the actions of a few evil people.

_____ Score 15 points for a correct M answer.

_____ Score 5 points for each correct B or N answer.

_____ **Total Score:** Finding the Main Idea

B | Recalling Facts

How well do you remember the facts in the article? Put an X in the box next to the answer that correctly completes each statement about the article.

1. Sarin attacks its victims'
   - ☐ a. lungs.
   - ☐ b. brains.
   - ☐ c. hearts.

2. The central train station was located near
   - ☐ a. a hospital.
   - ☐ b. police headquarters.
   - ☐ c. the airport.

3. Terrorists usually commit their acts to
   - ☐ a. make people pay attention to them.
   - ☐ b. start wars.
   - ☐ c. embarrass citizens.

4. This was *not* one of the powers Asahara claimed to have:
   - ☐ a. the ability to float in the air.
   - ☐ b. the ability to see the future.
   - ☐ c. the power to start fires with his mind only.

5. Asahara said that the most important weapon in the very last world war would be
   - ☐ a. mind control.
   - ☐ b. the atom bomb.
   - ☐ c. sarin.

Score 5 points for each correct answer.

_____ **Total Score:** Recalling Facts

C | Making Inferences

When you combine your own experience with information from a text to draw a conclusion that is not directly stated in that text, you are making an inference. Below are five statements that may or may not be inferences based on information in the article. Label the statements using the following key:

C—Correct Inference   **F—Faulty Inference**

_____ 1. It is common for people to leave lunch boxes behind on trains.

_____ 2. Asahara believed that he was becoming more powerful all the time.

_____ 3. The poison sarin affects everyone in exactly the same way.

_____ 4. As long as there are terrorists, no public place is perfectly safe.

_____ 5. Most people who followed Asahara were probably sensible and logical people.

> Score 5 points for each correct answer.
>
> _____ **Total Score:** Making Inferences

D | Using Words Precisely

Each numbered sentence below contains an underlined word or phrase from the article. Following the sentence are three definitions. One definition is closest to the meaning of the underlined word. One definition is opposite or nearly opposite. Label those two definitions using the following key; do not label the remaining definition.

C—Closest   **O—Opposite or Nearly Opposite**

1. That was what Tokyo's <u>commuters</u> were up against.

☐ a. machines

☐ b. people who work at home

☐ c. people who travel to and from jobs each day

2. The gas leaked out just as the three trains <u>converged on</u> the central station.

☐ a. met at

☐ b. took on passengers at

☐ c. branched off at

3. Newspapers from around the world <u>condemned</u> the attack.

☐ a. declared to be wrong or evil

☐ b. praised

☐ c. wrote about

4. One Japanese paper called it "mass murder" and "an <u>unthinkable</u> crime."

☐ a. easily understood

☐ b. unbelievable

☐ c. unsolved

5. The police then charged Asahara with <u>masterminding</u> the attack.

☐ a. knowing nothing about

☐ b. enjoying

☐ c. directing; organizing

_____ Score 3 points for each correct C answer.

_____ Score 2 points for each correct O answer.

_____ **Total Score:** Using Words Precisely

Enter the four total scores in the spaces below, and add them together to find your Reading Comprehension Score. Then record your score on the graph on page 149.

Score	Question Type	Lesson 15
_____	Finding the Main Idea	
_____	Recalling Facts	
_____	Making Inferences	
_____	Using Words Precisely	
_____	**Reading Comprehension Score**	

Author's Approach

Put an X in the box next to the correct answer.

1. What do the authors mean by the statement "The other [goal of the terrorists] was to thumb their noses at the police"?

☐ a. The terrorists wanted to show their support of the police.

☐ b. One of the terrorists' goals was to create a terrible smell for police to investigate.

☐ c. The terrorists wanted to prove that they could commit crimes freely, and the police could do nothing to stop them.

2. The main purpose of the first paragraph is to

☐ a. emphasize how clean and safe the Tokyo subway was.

☐ b. describe the workers on the Tokyo subway.

☐ c. persuade the reader to ride the Tokyo subway.

3. Which of the following statements from the article best describes one reason why police suspected Asahara of being behind the sarin attack?

☐ a. Asahara said that he could read people's minds.

☐ b. In his house, the police found materials needed to make sarin.

☐ c. He claimed he could see into the future.

4. From the statements below, choose those that you believe the authors would agree with.

☐ a. Tokyo is more dangerous than most big cities.

☐ b. People cannot feel perfectly safe anywhere.

☐ c. Asahara's teachings were very dangerous.

_____ Number of correct answers

Record your personal assessment of your work on the Critical Thinking Chart on page 150.

Summarizing and Paraphrasing

Follow the directions provided for question 1. Put an X in the box next to the correct answer for the other questions.

1. Look for the important ideas and events in paragraphs 16 and 17. Summarize those paragraphs in one or two sentences.

   _____

   _____

   _____

   _____

2. Below are summaries of the article. Choose the summary that says all the most important things about the article but in the fewest words.

   ☐ a. In 1995 a lethal chemical called sarin was planted on the Tokyo subway. It killed 12 passengers and sickened thousands of others. Police arrested Shoko Asahara for the crime. The head of a dangerous religious sect, he had predicted there would be a world war in which sarin was the main weapon.

   ☐ b. Terrorists used lunch boxes and soft drink bottles to sneak a dangerous chemical, sarin, onto the Tokyo subway in 1995. Sarin was invented in Germany in the 1930s. In its liquid and vapor forms, it could kill a human within minutes.

   ☐ c. The leader of a religious sect called "Supreme Truth" was Shoko Asahara. He boasted that he could read people's minds and see into the future. He claimed that the last world war would begin in 1997. Police blamed him for the 1995 sarin attack in Tokyo.

3. Choose the sentence that correctly restates the following sentence from the article "'Within a year,' [Asahara] predicted, 'my body should be able to fly at will.'"

   ☐ a. Within a year, Asahara began to claim that his body often willingly flew away.

   ☐ b. Asahara predicted that he would soon be able to fly anytime he wanted.

   ☐ c. Asahara said that although his body was willing to fly away, it was not able to do so at this time.

   ┌───┐
   │ _____ Number of correct answers   │
   │   │
   │ Record your personal assessment of your work on the │
   │ Critical Thinking Chart on page 150.   │
   └───┘

Critical Thinking

Put an X in the box next to the correct answer for the following questions.

1. Which of the following statements from the article is an opinion rather than a fact?

   ☐ a. He was the head of a religious sect known as the "Supreme Truth."

   ☐ b. Asahara had 10,000 followers in Japan.

   ☐ c. Such nonsense was pretty harmless.

2. From what the article said about Tokyo commuters' reaction to the sarin attack, you can predict that they

☐ a. have forgotten all about it by now.

☐ b. are still not sure about their safety on the subway.

☐ c. know that someone else is sure to terrorize the subway again.

3. What was the cause of the illness of thousands of commuters on the Tokyo subway on March 20, 1995?

☐ a. The commuters inhaled sarin in its vapor form.

☐ b. The commuters panicked over the possibility of a terrorist attack.

☐ c. The commuters swallowed sarin in its liquid form.

4. How is "Death Rides the Subway" related to the theme of this book?

☐ a. Commuters panicked when they suddenly discovered that they all felt sick and weak.

☐ b. One man was able to persuade people to commit a terrible crime.

☐ c. A subway worker died only hours after picking up a small package filled with the lethal chemical sarin.

5. What did you have to do to answer question 2?

☐ a. find an opinion (what someone thinks about something)

☐ b. make a prediction (what might happen next)

☐ c. find a cause (why something happened)

_____ Number of correct answers

Record your personal assessment of your work on the Critical Thinking Chart on page 150.

Personal Response

This article is different from other articles about events that caused panic I've read because _____

_____

And Asahara is unlike other criminals because _____

_____

_____

_____

Self-Assessment

A word or phrase in the article that I do not understand is _____

_____

_____

Compare and Contrast

Think about the articles you have read in Unit Three. Pick the three events that you would have found most frightening. Write the titles of the articles that tell about them in the first column of the chart below. Use information you learned from the articles to fill in the empty boxes in the chart.

Title	When did the victims realize they were in danger?	What steps did authorities take to help the public?	What parts of this situation did you find most frightening?

Imagine that you are in the situation described in the article _____

Write two or three entries from your daily journal. _____

_____

_____

Words-per-Minute Table

Unit Three

Directions: If you were timed while reading an article, refer to the Reading Time you recorded in the box at the end of the article. Use this Words-per-Minute Table to determine your reading speed for that article. Then plot your reading speed on the graph on page 148.

Lesson	11	12	13	14	15	
No. of Words	1,013	1,191	1,121	1,080	1,049	
1:30	675	794	747	720	699	**90**
1:40	608	715	673	648	629	**100**
1:50	553	650	611	589	572	**110**
2:00	507	596	561	540	525	**120**
2:10	468	550	517	498	484	**130**
2:20	434	510	480	463	450	**140**
2:30	405	476	448	432	420	**150**
2:40	380	447	420	405	393	**160**
2:50	358	420	396	381	370	**170**
3:00	338	397	374	360	350	**180**
3:10	320	376	354	341	331	**190**
3:20	304	357	336	324	315	**200**
3:30	289	340	320	309	300	**210**
3:40	276	325	306	295	286	**220**
3:50	264	311	292	282	274	**230**
4:00	253	298	280	270	262	**240**
4:10	243	286	269	259	252	**250**
4:20	234	275	259	249	242	**260**
4:30	225	265	249	240	233	**270**
4:40	217	255	240	231	225	**280**
4:50	210	246	232	223	217	**290**
5:00	203	238	224	216	210	**300**
5:10	196	231	217	209	203	**310**
5:20	190	223	210	203	197	**320**
5:30	184	217	204	196	191	**330**
5:40	179	210	198	191	185	**340**
5:50	174	204	192	185	180	**350**
6:00	169	199	187	180	175	**360**
6:10	164	193	182	175	170	**370**
6:20	160	188	177	171	166	**380**
6:30	156	183	172	166	161	**390**
6:40	152	179	168	162	157	**400**
6:50	148	174	164	158	154	**410**
7:00	145	170	160	154	150	**420**
7:10	141	166	156	151	146	**430**
7:20	138	162	153	147	143	**440**
7:30	135	159	149	144	140	**450**
7:40	132	155	146	141	137	**460**
7:50	129	152	143	138	134	**470**
8:00	127	149	140	135	131	**480**

Minutes and Seconds

Seconds

Plotting Your Progress: Reading Speed

Unit Three

Directions: If you were timed while reading an article, write your words-per-minute rate for that article in the box under the number of the lesson. Then plot your reading speed on the graph by putting a small X on the line directly above the number of the lesson, across from the number of words per minute you read. As you mark your speed for each lesson, graph your progress by drawing a line to connect the X's.

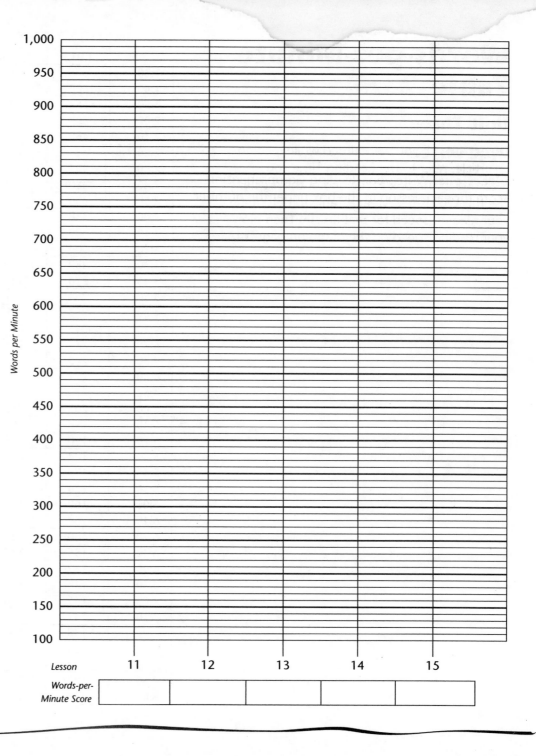

Lesson	11	12	13	14	15
Words-per-Minute Score					

Plotting Your Progress: Reading Comprehension

Unit Three

Directions: Write your Reading Comprehension Score for each lesson in the box under the number of the lesson. Then plot your score on the graph by putting a small X on the line directly above the number of the lesson and across from the score you earned. As you mark your score for each lesson, graph your progress by drawing a line to connect the X's.

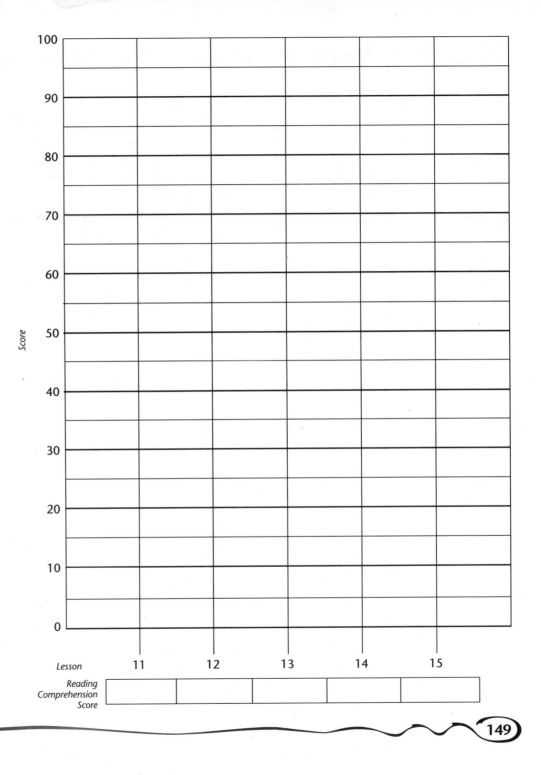

Plotting Your Progress: Critical Thinking

Unit Three

Directions: Work with your teacher to evaluate your responses to the Critical Thinking questions for each lesson. Then fill in the appropriate spaces in the chart below. For each lesson and each type of Critical Thinking question, do the following: Mark a minus sign (–) in the box to indicate areas in which you feel you could improve. Mark a plus sign (+) to indicate areas in which you feel you did well. Mark a minus-slash-plus sign (–/+) to indicate areas in which you had mixed success. Then write any comments you have about your performance, including ideas for improvement.

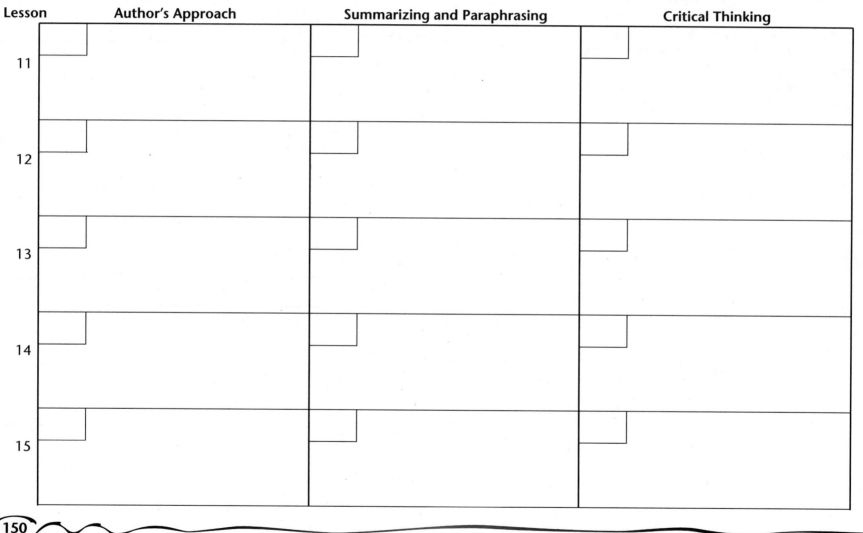

Lesson	Author's Approach	Summarizing and Paraphrasing	Critical Thinking
11			
12			
13			
14			
15			

Photo Credits